A BUSINESSMAN LOOKS AT THE BIBLE

A BUSINESSMAN LOOKS AT THE BIBLE

W. Maxey Jarman

FLEMING H. REVELL COMPANY
WESTWOOD, NEW JERSEY

Preface

Any person who is in a position of leadership has an obligation to let people know where he stands. If he has convictions and integrity, he should make those convictions known without being obnoxious about it.

The general impression of many people these days is that the Bible is an outmoded Book of questionable value in today's modern, scientific, materialistic world. It is a Book to have but not necessarily to read, is the apparent general opinion. With these viewpoints I strongly disagree and in this book I offer my observations on this Book of books. Since my chief occupation has been with the business world, this observation represents a layman's personal investigation and experience with a Book that I believe to be absolutely unique in every way. I am of course referring to its message and not to the form of the Bible itself.

My business career has been entirely with one company. It was started by my father, James Franklin Jarman, and William Hatch Wemyss in 1924. I started when the business did, as a very young and green kid. The business began in a small way with $130,000 in capital and 120 employees. Today it has more than $150 million in capital and about 45,000 employees.

During the same years that I have had an interesting business career, I have also had many interesting experiences in my spiritual life. I have been active in church and denominational life and in various other religious activities. I have probably learned more about the Bible in trying to teach it to others than in any other way. My first experiences in teaching the Bible were with a group of fourteen-year-old boys. Anybody who has tried to hold the attention of a group of active boys and at the same time teach them something about the Bible has to learn a lot himself. It is gratifying, however, to see what has happened to some of those boys—one of them now serving as president of the Southern Baptist Convention.

This book is not written to say that the Bible has helped me to be a success in business. I believe that strong character is one of the essentials in business success and that a deep religious experience will help produce strength of character. But character is only the foundation; business success requires many other qualifications in addition. I have seen many people who had deep and sincere and sound religious convictions but who did not have the other qualifications for business success.

Furthermore, business success is not necessarily success in living. I have known many people with small incomes who lived a more successful life than some business executives who had large incomes.

This book, then, is the expression of one businessman about the Bible. The personal facts that I have included are only for the purpose of giving the background of my approach to believing and understanding the Bible. It is a businessman's statement, not a theologian's.

It would be impossible to acknowledge all of those who have influenced me and helped me to understand my own attitudes and convictions. I would like particularly to express appreciation of those who have listened to me try to teach the Bible, of my pastors and church associates, of my father and mother.

My wife has been patient and a source of great encouragement and inspiration. Mrs. Phyllis Murphy has been marvelously helpful in the editing of the manuscript, and Miss Margie Keith, my business assistant, has been most cooperative in the preparation.

My especial thanks to God for the privilege of serving Him, and I pray for His blessings on any who read this message.

W. MAXEY JARMAN

Nashville, Tennessee

Contents

Contents

A BUSINESSMAN LOOKS AT THE BIBLE

1

What About the Word?

Is the Bible the real Word of God? The answer a man gives to that question can have a lot to do with his life. The kind of life a person leads, the actions he takes, the mental security he finds are determined by the basic beliefs he holds.

The Bible has come to us through centuries of efforts to suppress it, destroy it, and laugh at it. This Book has caused men to suffer and die for it, and has given others an amazing joy. It makes strange claims for itself.

If there is a God and if this Book reveals Him to us, as it claims, we would be foolish indeed to ignore it, to neglect to know what the Creator of the universe would tell us. But how can we answer those two questions: Is there a God?—and does the Bible reveal Him to us?

I was raised in a religious family, and from early childhood I had impressed upon me that God was my heavenly Father and that the Bible was the inspired Book that told men about God. But most young people arrive at an age when they begin to question everything, and I was no exception.

I thought about that question of the truth of the

Bible for some time. It was such an important one that I had to find the answer for myself. I am inclined to be somewhat stubborn and independent, and I was not going to let somebody else decide whether or not I could appreciate and understand the Bible. Here was a tangible document that anybody could examine. If it were true, then it would help to give me an authoritative answer to the question about the existence of God. If, after fair and thorough consideration, I should happen to decide that it was just another book, the time spent would not be a calamity, for I would have learned more than most people know about a very important Book in the history of mankind.

We do not know much about the origin or history of the Bible. We know it is one of the most ancient books we have, and it was compiled by many human writers over a period of many centuries. The Old Testament came to us through the Israelites and the New Testament came through the disciples of Jesus, the Jews who knew Him when He walked the earth in the flesh more than nineteen hundred years ago. Although many of those men were relatively uneducated, by divine inspiration they were able to put together words that have glowed with life through the ages. But the Bible is not a human book in the ordinary sense of the word; it is a supernatural Book. Its preservation, its unity, its concept, and most of all its power testify to its unusual character and uniqueness.

My experience in business has taught me that a man must constantly search for facts if he wants to make the proper decisions. He must test each item of information that comes into his office if he is to learn what each one means, which ones are important, and which ones do not stack up after being double-checked.

This is also a part of the methodology of science. Any researcher continually tests his information to find the truth. He experiments with tentative conclusions to see whether they work out in practice. It is this search for truth that is the basis for success in any endeavor.

In my business—designing, manufacturing, and distributing all kinds of things that people wear—I have learned that when an idea is presented, it must be tested in practice, not just discussed in theory. Before a new product is put on the market, its raw materials must first be checked and spot-tested to find out whether they come up to standards. There are several machines used in this procedure, but the most important test is the "feel" of the material in the experienced hands of someone who can determine its quality. As a product is made, it is inspected at various stages, and each of the hundreds of different operations is checked daily. Through years of experience, a manufacturer is able to establish standards of workmanship, and it is against these criteria that each item and each operation is carefully checked.

When a new item of apparel or footwear is finished, it meets its toughest test. It has to be worn over a period of time. Here, too, we need people. The size dimensions of clothing are important because each individual varies from each other individual in some of his measurements. His dimensions also change when he moves, if he gains or loses weight, during summer and winter, and under many other conditions. For these and other reasons a new product has to be wear-tested many times by many people, under varying conditions, and in different geographical locations. All these tests require a lot of time, study, and experience, but the results are well worth while.

These methods are routine in business, and they were the best tools I had at my command. I decided to use them to test the Bible.

I knew that my first step was to become thoroughly familiar with the Bible. That is easy to say and not too difficult to do with most books. But the Bible is different from other books, and I knew I faced a hard task, to say the least. I do not mean that I agree with those who say the Bible cannot be understood by ordinary people. It has not lived through nineteen centuries because it is an obscure Book. It has been understood by all kinds of people, educated and uneducated, highly intellectual people and "just average" people—and even some who were not so average. The Bible's message can be understood by anyone who approaches it with a fair attitude.

After learning as much as possible about the Book, I would have to put into practice some of the things I had learned in business. For example, a successful business executive must be realistic. He must probe deeply, ask penetrating questions, and be sure that he has heard and considered both the favorable and unfavorable points of a given matter. He may appear to be suspicious and hardboiled in his efforts to look at all sides, but he has learned, often from bitter experience, not to go easy in digging for all the facts so that he can weigh them objectively.

A businessman is by nature a practical man, and I knew I would be asking another question—Is the Bible just a theoretical Book, or does it have practical applications to life today? I had to find out how the Bible influenced other people, what it had to say about all the different kinds of circumstances men meet today. I wanted to know whether the Bible really works—and if it does, why?

When I am looking for an answer to a business problem, I am usually aware of my limitations, and I frequently call in specialists to consider the factors involved. But I have also been taught by experience that, while experts are helpful, their ideas and recommendations can rarely be used exactly as they are presented. They are most valuable as a stimulating influence. In approaching my study of the Bible, I decided to keep my mind open to the views of the experts, but I was going to check their views with the Book itself.

Perhaps I went to work with a prejudiced point of view, but I believe that the techniques used in the business world are particularly well suited to an analysis of the Bible. If I was going to search for an answer to the question, "Is the Bible true?" I would have to follow my project through to completion; I had learned the value of persistence. I would have to separate the parts of my study according to their timing, relative importance, and interrelationship to each other; I was familiar with the practice of taking both a short- and long-term view.

Although businessmen use certain general approaches when analyzing a project, the personal viewpoints of each individual executive will influence the final decision. This was certainly true of me. The personal facts of my life were going to have a bearing on my entire study of the Bible, and I realized that I would have to examine them as well.

t Route

hurch every Sunday and
m my allowance. My life
was carefully restricted as to amusements and worldly
activities.

As a family we read from the Bible at breakfast every
morning and I was often exposed to conversation about
it. I accepted it without question then, just as I accepted food, clothing, and shelter from my family.
When I was eleven I had a conversion experience and
became a member of our church, which was affiliated
with the Southern Baptist Convention.

Slowly building up within me, however, was a feeling of resentment toward the restrictions that kept me
from the things most of my acquaintances were doing.
And as I progressed in my education, questions began
to crop up about matters I had once accepted with
complete confidence.

I had deep respect for my family. I knew that my
father was a man of the highest principles and an excel-
lent student of the Bible. But I began to wonder

whether my parents were somewhat out of date and not quite up on modern things. Doesn't that sound normal? I think that most people, if they level with themselves, will remember when they first began to feel somewhat superior to their parents. I've often wished that I could be half as smart now as I thought I was when I was twenty years old.

I was away from home for the first time when I was admitted to Massachusetts Institute of Technology— which I believe is still the foremost scientific and engineering educational institution in the world. But the change in my environment was a rough experience for a sensitive seventeen-year-old who had been carefully protected all his life. I was in a different part of the country, among people I did not know. I was exposed to a different kind of church, came into contact with agnostics, skeptics, and atheists, many of them intellectually brilliant, who seemed to take delight in ridiculing a young, unsophisticated person who did not know how to answer them or turn aside their jibes. I realize now that I was going through a conflict that catches up with many young people at some stage in their lives.

It was during those years at college that I began to feel a need to find out whether the Bible was truly the Word of God. Religion was constantly discussed in the fraternity house, and I found I couldn't answer a lot of the questions that came up. I still don't know whether it was through obstinacy or God-given faith, but I managed to stand my ground in those discussions, even though it took some bluffing at times. I couldn't help noticing, too, that although I didn't have all the answers, a lot of the skeptics weren't so sure of theirs. As I look back now, I think they wanted to destroy someone else's faith because they had none of their own and somehow realized that there was a big empty place in their lives.

As I struggled for some answers, I found that the most dangerous attacks on my youthful faith came not from skeptics, but from so-called religious people who did not fully accept the Bible as truth and who tried to rationalize its concepts into some kind of conformity with their own views of life. In the days of Jesus Christ, His harshest condemnation fell upon the Pharisees, the pseudoreligious "do-gooders" who appeared to the world as religious leaders but who in truth had no faith at all. Christ used strong language to describe them— ". . . hypocrites, . . . whited sepulchres, . . . full of dead men's bones, . . . fools, . . . blind guides, . . . serpents, . . . vipers. . . ." We have too many of the same kind of religious people today, and I am sure that if Christ were to appear in the flesh now, He would condemn them in the same words.

The problem of whom to believe and whom not to believe is one that every mature person faces constantly. As I began to probe and reason and expose the fallacies in another man's argument, I realized that it was better to try to think clearly about important matters than to accept someone else's opinion. If I were to accept the opinions of the apparently sophisticated people in my new environment, it meant that I would have to throw out everything my family had taught me.

But if I could no longer accept my father's ideas, why should I accept the ideas of these new people? Did they have any more access to real truth than my father? Was it possible that both were wrong? How could I decide which route to take?

In mathematics we are taught to prove our answers, to know whether we are right or wrong. Theorems in geometry are based on logical proof. Was it possible to find similar approaches to spiritual matters? These were some of the questions that were going through my mind at that time. Unfortunately, too many people push aside these questions, or they accept a different set of beliefs based on the opinions of people who seem to be in the majority. Actually, a majority opinion is often wrong because so many people do not think for themselves.

When does one decide to think for himself? The process probably begins in childhood, and if it is encouraged it can strengthen a man's determination to probe for facts on his own, to examine the opinions that other people toss out so glibly. It can also be suffocated before it gets very far.

While my independent attitude and questioning mind may have made me unpopular with some people, they have helped me to learn a lot. Your belief should be your own—not mine or another person's. This is what Paul commended when he spoke about the people of Berea who studied the Scriptures for themselves and checked everything he told them.

In my search for facts on which to base my beliefs I attended various churches. I found that the expressed beliefs of some of them did not hang together; others made deep impressions on me and encouraged me to check with the Bible to see whether they were quoting correctly. Whenever I went home, I asked questions, and a few people who had made intensive studies of the Bible opened my eyes to some things I had not understood. Because I was checking their beliefs as well as others', I did not discuss the matter with my family to any extent. I am sure, however, that they were aware of some of the problems that were bothering me. I am sure, too, that their prayers made a powerful impact on my spiritual nature.

While I was beginning to learn about the Bible, I was learning about the business world as well. I had started to work in my father's company when I was twenty years old, and at twenty-eight I became its president when my father's health began to fail. Although I expect to keep on learning as long as I live, I think those first few years of experience were the most important ones in my business career. But it was not until I began to teach a Sunday school class of fourteen-year-old boys that I really started to learn something about people and the Bible. It took digging to find the answers to the questions those boys asked, and they taught me a lot.

Later I found that there were other men with questions, too. Two hundred of us formed a study group, and for fifteen years I served as teacher in one of the most rewarding activities of my life. A person gets to know himself by working with other people. Getting up in front of a lot of intelligent, realistic, sometimes skeptical men every week and giving them something to think about means that you have to do some hard work in the Bible.

Perhaps because I am a businessman I am partial to a direct, straightforward approach to the Bible. But I firmly believe that it is more meaningful than the kind of approach that gets bogged down in a morass of theory or one that is sketchy and haphazard. A person who wants to find out about the truth of the Bible can study its history, learn about its various writers, investigate the way its parts were put together; he can review the various translations and read all the literature on the subject. But the best way to learn the Bible is to go to the Book.

3

A Better Way to Read

Many years ago, when I first read the Bible through, I had no comprehension of great portions of it, but I can remember that the experience was rewarding. During the past forty years I have read the Bible through every year, and my rewards have increased.

For one thing, I have learned how to discipline myself so that I allow time to read a portion of the Bible every day. This has given me a feeling of satisfaction, a kind of peace of mind. I have also trained myself to read fast because I want to read as many books as possible during my lifetime. It's a good habit, and I find that I retain much more than I did as a slow reader —possibly because I have to concentrate on what I am reading if I want to keep up my pace. Still, the Bible is a long Book, and reading it through takes a good deal of time.

John P. Holmes, a former vice president of the Celanese Corporation, said, "Each time I read and study the New Testament, I find new revelations" (Wallace Speers, *Laymen Speaking*), and I believe that to be true of the whole Book. Year after year more passages become familiar, yet something new and fresh seems to pop out from them. It might be in the form of a new approach to a current question in my life, a deeper insight into a problem, or perhaps a beautiful expression that suddenly seems to reach into the heart of the soul.

The Bible has a lot to say about how we should read it, and it states quite clearly that its message will not be understood by those who take pride in their intellectual capacities. While it is profound and deep, it is designed to be understood by anyone who approaches it with humility, an open mind, and a sincere desire to learn the truth. I have tried to follow these directions in my approach to a study of the Bible. When I asked myself, "Can I really hope to have a revelation of divine power?" I found that I undertook my job with humility.

A newborn baby desires milk without understanding why he wants it or what it will do for him, and that is the way the Bible tells us it should be read. How can a baby know that milk will be converted into muscle, blood, gland-building and brain-developing energy for his growing body? How much do we really know about the growth of the personality, the development of the soul and spirit, the concepts of faith and love within us? And who can understand how spiritual things work when he can't even understand how physical things work? When I began to read the Bible, I had only a dim comprehension of its real value, but I had a burning desire to know what it contained, and I read its words as a baby absorbs milk. I have since learned that even though we may not learn how they work, these words will influence our hearts and souls and lives.

If a person wants to understand the teachings of the Bible, he should first begin to live according to those teachings, for the Bible tells us that understanding will follow action. I decided that I would try, to the best of my ability, to live according to the principles I was about to discover. Some people may think that is too big a price to pay for an experiment in truth, but I was willing to pay it. Speaking from a business viewpoint, I think the price is very low indeed, considering the results a man can achieve.

4

The Test Begins

The Bible invites testing. It encourages the sincere seeker to claim its promises, to try its methods, to check its results. But how does one conduct such a test?

The routine tests of the business world cannot be used on the whole Bible, for some of its parts cannot be tested directly. Human beings have finite minds and they can understand only those things that come within the range of their minds. Beyond that, men can speculate. For example, we speculate about whether or not there is any form of life on other planets; but we will not know for sure until we can visit those planets.

There are some matters on which men cannot even speculate. Does our universe have an outer boundary? If so, what lies beyond outer space? If our minds cannot grasp the concepts of limitless space, how can we comprehend such things as eternity or infinity?

Of course, man is endowed with reason, and he can come to some logical conclusions about certain abstract ideas. For centuries man has been observing the phenomena in the world about him and formulating theories about the causes of them. But for just as many centuries many of his theories have been proved wrong because his observations were incomplete or his reasoning erroneous.

The whole idea of God is such a matter. Man can speculate on whether or not there is a God and he can try to reach a conclusion about the nature of God. He can even come to have convictions about the matter. But man of his own direct knowledge cannot determine whether or not there is a God. If he takes a position about the existence of God, his conviction must be based on something we call "faith," and this becomes a stumbling block to a great many people.

The person who decides that there is no God is acting on faith just as much as the person who decides that God exists. Perhaps it is a different kind of faith, but his decision is based on his assumptions and feelings, not on external proof. His opinion causes him to live a life that is entirely different from the life of a person who believes that God exists, and if he is wrong he has paid a big price for his mistake.

Agnostics say that we cannot be certain whether or not there is a God. Many of them, emphasizing the limitations of the human mind in comprehending the infinite, push aside the question without ever giving it consideration. I have known a number of agnostics, but I have never known one to make a serious, openminded attempt to look for the answer in the Bible.

I am always surprised, in this day of scientific marvels, when people question the existence of faith. The fact that we use and enjoy such things as electricity, gravity, television, atomic energy, is evidence that human beings can accept things they do not understand. So it is with spiritual matters—faith can accept the things that work without understanding how they work.

Many parts of the Bible deal with concepts that are well within the scope of the human mind, however, and these can be tested directly.

Although it does not claim to be a textbook on scientific subjects, the Bible refers to many natural events and claims to speak the truth about them. I have read a lot of the literature on this subject, enough to convince myself that modern studies in geology, astronomy, biology, history, and other sciences stand as witnesses to the Bible's claim.

Geologists know, for example, that great cataclysmic changes have occurred on our planet. They also know that the earth has existed for more thousands of years than we can imagine, although they cannot tell us when the beginning was, how the earth was created, or what power created it. The Bible tells us simply and directly: "In the beginning God created the heavens and earth. . . ." It also tells us that the earth was changed from its original creation: ". . . and the earth had become waste and wild" (ROTHERHAM).

Another example of the Bible's accuracy is a passage in Isaiah (40:22): "He sits over the round earth, so high that its inhabitants look like grasshoppers" (MOFFATT). These words were written centuries ago when people thought the earth was flat.

When very minor details of Scripture are found to be true, it gives me great confidence in the validity of the whole Book. On such detail is an incident dealing with the death of Jezebel. On the orders of Jehu, Jezebel was thrown from a palace window into the courtyard below, where horses trampled her body. Later, when Jehu ordered her remains to be buried, his men found that the dogs had eaten all but her skull, feet, and the palms of her hands. Why didn't the dogs devour her completely? The Bible offers no explanation; it simply records what happened, horrible as it was. Centuries later, the answer came from cannibals whom missionaries had taught to read the Bible. They understood the significance of the details of Jezebel's story and explained that the feet and the palms of the hands were never eaten because they are very bitter.

Historians as well as Bible students have been interested in the large portions of Scripture that deal with the descendants of Jacob, whose name was changed to Israel. The fact that the Jews have continued as a separate people wherever they have lived, and that they exist as they do today, is a powerful confirmation of the Bible's prophecy regarding them. Perhaps no other people have been so persecuted; perhaps no other people have made such a mark on civilization.

The downfall of Babylon is one of many Biblical prophecies that have already come true. Babylon at the height of her glory was a walled city of great wealth and power; her hanging gardens were among the seven wonders of the ancient world. It was amid that setting that Jeremiah the Prophet, under the inspiration of God, predicted her fate: ". . . none shall remain in it, neither man nor beast, but that it shall be desolate for ever" (51:62, KJV).

When I was in Baghdad a few years ago, I rented a car and a driver and rode ninety miles to see what was left of the great city. The ruins are there and the prophecy has come true. No one lives in Babylon now, and it is one of the most desolate places I have ever seen. We could apply the test to many other astounding prophecies in the Bible and find that they too are correct.

Some people say that the Bible contradicts itself and therefore cannot be accepted as the Word of God. Actually it would be almost unnatural if we did not find contradictions in such a long Book, written in several ancient languages, by so many different people, over such a long period of years. Of course, it would be impossible for me to say that I have examined every possible situation; but I am convinced, after much study, that I have not found any contradictions in concept or expression. In fact, I think the Bible's unity offers impressive evidence of its validity. Consider the fact that the symbolism shows up in the same manner, place after place; the central theme is consistent, straight through from start to finish; one part throws light on the other, with mysteries in the Old Testament being made clear in the New Testament.

Yes, there are apparent contradictions if one approaches the Bible looking for something to criticize, ready to pounce on anything that does not seem right. If someone is sure beforehand that the Bible *can't* be true, then he will certainly find some things to talk about.

If, however, a person approaches the Bible with a

sympathetic viewpoint, he will not throw up his hands when he finds something that does not seem to fit into the whole. He will explore the matter until he finds the explanation. That has been my approach, and every difficulty that I have studied has yielded a satisfactory explanation in time.

There are several reasons why the Bible is accused of being contradictory, and they can all be attributed to people rather than Scripture. Some of the misunderstanding has been caused by those who try to make the Bible say what they think it should say. But the Bible cannot be used to fit into man's human desires or moral standards. When people close their minds to the complete message, they humanize the Word to the point of confusion.

Those who quote Scripture out of context often create the very contradictions they point out. The Bible does not lend itself to piecemeal use, and we cannot take certain parts that we like and omit the others. Critics who interpret some passages apart from the rest of the Book end up by interpreting themselves. If they would study the complete Word, they would find that the Bible is its own best interpreter.

The Bible uses all kinds of figures of speech to get its concepts across to those who want to understand. Sometimes it uses a paradox, a figure of speech which presents a seeming contradiction but a basic truth. Sometimes it speaks in parables, such as those told by Jesus, so that only those with the right key will be able to unlock the door to understanding. People who are trying to discredit the Bible are perplexed by these figures of speech and do not go on to learn the deeper truth they hold.

A reader with an open mind can and should test the Bible for scientific and historical accuracy; he should examine the unfolding of its prophecies; he should become thoroughly familiar with the interrelationship of the parts that make up the whole—for only then can he begin to find understanding. The reader with a closed mind is wasting his time. He will become lost in the midst of the truth he refuses to recognize.

5

How Does the Bible Wear?

When a retailer is approached by a manufacturer who wants him to take on a line of merchandise he has not previously handled, the retailer subjects the sample products to a lot of tests to determine their salability. He also listens to the manufacturer's claims, finds out about prices and terms, and tries to decide whether the whole proposition seems sensible. If the merchandise does not come up to the retailer's standards of quality, it is rejected. If the manufacturer's salesman makes unreasonable claims or contradicts himself in his presentation, then it is unlikely that the retailer will place any orders.

But, assuming all these tests are favorable, the retailer will still want to know what experience others have had with the products. Even when a salesman refers to merchants who have had success with his merchandise, the retailer may want to get a firsthand report.

The Bible must be tested in the same way. If it seems to be true on the basis of testing its facts and checking its consistency, the next step is to test it in practice. What experiences have other people had with it? How does the Bible wear?

Not all people can testify to the same results. Some accept the Bible in part and reject it in part; some reject it altogether; some accept it wholly and believe in it.

I have talked with people who accept only those parts of the Bible that seem to tie in with their personal philosophy of God, and I have observed that the Bible does not touch their lives in a deeply significant way. Most of them would say that it is a great Book, but it does not carry much weight with them. It is somewhat surprising to learn that many of these people are students of the Bible—for example, some seminary students. But their approach has been entirely intellectual, and therefore they have missed the message.

I do not mean to infer that an intellectual person is incapable of understanding the Bible, for this is far from true. I believe that his task will be more difficult. Yet, many intellectuals have completely accepted the Bible and acknowledge that their lives have been changed by it.

There are people who reject the whole Bible, but most of them have neither read it completely nor seriously considered its teachings. I expect that some of them have "tried" the Bible and then given it up. I do not believe that I have ever known anyone who reached maturity with a conviction about the truth of the Bible, or who accepted it after reaching maturity, and later turned away from it.

Among those who accept the Bible, believe in it, and

try to live according to its teachings, I have found two groups. The larger group believe that the Bible is true because their parents taught them to believe in it or because they never lived in an atmosphere where it was doubted. Their belief is not based upon their own examination, and many have never even read the whole Book. Those of this group who have read it demonstrate no real understanding of it.

A small number of people make up the second group. They have studied the Bible, they believe in its validity, and their lives give evidence of its influence on them.

I have had the opportunity to know many people of all types, and I have discovered that the real users of the Bible give the most convincing testimonials to their experience with it. Generally they constitute a delightful and stimulating group, and as I think of the people I have known who have fine character, I realize that many of them are those with strong religious convictions.

When a person has a deep experience with the Bible and comes to accept its truth, it can change his life. I know a man who grew up in Australia, was studying to be a priest in another faith, and at the age of eighteen had never seen the Bible. Quite accidentally he came across a portion of it, and it so intrigued him that he got a copy of the whole Book. After studying it he was convinced of its truth, and he left his home to go to South America where he began to live a new life based upon what the Bible had taught him. His experience could be multiplied many times.

Going back to the analogy of the retailer—if he

learns that a new line of merchandise has produced outstanding results for those who have used it, then his decision will certainly be a favorable one. Having arrived at the conclusion that the claims of the new product are valid, his next step is to take action, to make a commitment, to use the merchandise in the proper way. It is not too hard to study a matter objectively, but when it comes to making an investment in it or changing a method of production, a certain amount of risk is involved. The retailer, in other words, has come to the point where he must have enough faith in the product to take the risk.

The same thing applies to a study of the Bible. Anyone seeking to determine the truth of the Bible comes to a point where he must begin to accept its truth if he is going to test it out in his own life.

What risks are involved if I accept the Bible as truth and commit my life to its teachings? There are several. First of all, if I am wrong about my conclusions, then I won't know it until I am dead. And even then I won't really know, because if I am wrong my existence will end with my physical death. But I also run a risk if I refuse to accept the Bible as truth. And if I am wrong on that basis, I probably *will* know about it after I am dead—and it will be too late to do anything about it. I must risk a lifetime or an eternity.

Suppose I accept the Bible and it turns out that I am wrong? What have I lost? What has it cost me during my life on earth? A lot of people will say that I have given up a lot of fun, but I cannot agree with them. I have never found anything in the Bible that prohibits me from enjoying myself. Rather, I find many promises of the finest values in life. True, I have seen some Bible-believers who do not seem to be having much fun, but I have seen others who are enjoying life to the fullest.

One such person is a business acquaintance of mine who puts complete faith in the Bible, as do I. This man is successful in his business, an active sportsman, and a diligent worker in church affairs. He travels a lot, for both business and pleasure, has a grand sense of humor, a delightful personality, many friends, and a happy family. He has also memorized many passages of Scripture—an accomplishment I particularly admire, perhaps because I find it so difficult. Although he and I would not agree on every point in the interpretation of the Bible, we both know that we wholeheartedly accept it as truth. And I cannot see where his acceptance has taken the joy out of his life.

Of course, people have different definitions of enjoyment and different ways of seeking it. But I cannot convince myself that "hell-raising" is a good route to enjoying life, nor have I observed that "doing what comes naturally" produces any lasting satisfaction.

Another possible risk I take is that I might be wasting my time. After all, accepting the Bible means that I must put a considerable amount of my time into religious activity, and many people might say that my time could be put to better use in developing my mind, enlarging my business, improving my cultural level, enjoying my family and friends, or just taking my leisure. But it has not been necessary for me to give up any of these things.

The use of time is a fascinating subject to me. Everybody has the same number of hours each day, but some people seem to get a lot more out of their share. I first became aware of the importance of time when I was in college, and I realized there were so many things I wanted to do but so little time to do them. So I decided that I would allocate my hours each day so as to use them more productively. I must confess that although I have tried to use my hours well these many years, I still find myself wasting many of them on matters of little importance which yield few satisfactory results.

Curiously, it is the people who put a lot of time into religious activity who also seem to have more time for family, business, sports, travel, reading, and many other pursuits. Show me any number of individuals who seem to get a lot out of their twenty-four hours a day, and I believe I can easily match them with Bible-believers who get as much and even more out of their day. Perhaps the hours a man spends on religious activity actually make it possible for him to make better use of time.

All of us waste time, sometimes through our own carelessness, sometimes through things beyond our control; but there are many little ways of making the hours count for something. One good device is to write down every evening the matters that should be given priority the next day. By analyzing the ways in which he spends his days, a man can find out how to use the odd moments, the little minutes of waiting for someone.

Perhaps the most important way to get the best use from our time is to make right decisions and to make them promptly. Indecisiveness and rehashing of past decisions are not only time-wasters but bad habits. Wrong decisions certainly waste time, too, and they are damaging in many other ways.

If we are going to make right decisions, make them quicker, and not worry about them after they are made, we are going to need some spiritual insight and wisdom. Decisions involve an estimation of people, an assumption about future developments, and weighing of relative values. If he depends solely upon his own mental equipment, knowledge, and experience, no human being can make truly effective decisions. We need the help and guidance of a higher power if we are to get the most from our twenty-four hours a day. That help is available, for Jesus said that He came into the world that we might have a fuller, richer life.

I suppose some people might think I am also taking a risk by investing some money in religious activities when I could be spending it in a dozen other ways. I have a pretty strong feeling about the danger of money and the desire for wealth. Money has a strong appeal to almost everyone, and the love of it can creep up on us until it takes command of our lives. There are so many delectable things we would like to buy, so many urgent needs. But money is a hard taskmaster. It demands its pound of flesh and takes its toll in blood, sweat, and tears.

Money should properly be our servant, and each of us needs something to prevent it from becoming our master. By developing the habit of giving our money to religious causes and various other worthy causes, we can tear ourselves loose from our eager taskmaster and build stronger characters. It won't do to tell ourselves that a good portion of our tax money goes to good causes. When we pay our taxes we are doing something required of us, and nothing in that will strengthen our character. When we give our money voluntarily, we are doing something we are not required to do, and we grow through the experience.

I considered all these risks a long time ago, and I decided to take them. I had come to the conclusion that the weight of all the evidence called for an acceptance of the Bible as truth. I then had to make my commitment.

I have committed myself to accepting the truth of the whole Bible—including those parts that I do not understand as yet. In my business, if I am convinced by the evidence that an electronic data-processing machine will perform certain functions, I am ready to rely on that machine even though I do not understand how it works. The results count.

My commitment means that when I find something in the Bible that doesn't jibe with my experience, I will assume the Bible to be correct and my experience unreliable. Certainly I want to explore the ideas I find in the Bible so that I will not get mixed up about them, but I begin my exploration with the conviction that the Bible is true. After all, I would not need the Bible or any other source of truth if I could rely on the validity of my own knowledge and experience. This I cannot do, for I have found that such self-reliance has frequently gotten me into trouble. Furthermore, there are so many things beyond my ability to imagine, that I am convinced of my need for a divine revelation of God and a dependent relationship with Him.

Since I made my personal commitment many years ago, my relationship to the Bible has grown more satisfying each year. There have been times, of course, when doubts entered my mind and I needed a new reassurance of my faith in the Book. At times, too, some of the passages seemed distasteful or irrelevant to my life and the modern world. But I continued in my commitment, and those occasions did not last long. Eventually, as my doubts and objections were eliminated, I came to know an even greater love and respect for the Book I know as the Word of God.

When a person accepts the Bible with reservations, it becomes just another book, and religion becomes a philosophy of life, a code of ethics. It is fine to have a philosophy and to live by a code of ethics, but they do not in any way take the place of religious faith. When faith comes first, all other matters of life fall into place.

An acceptance of the Bible as truth leaves open the many questions of interpretation. It is true that the Bible was originally written in various ancient languages and that proper translation is not easy because the meaning of the words has changed over the centuries. New translations are needed from time to time, and some of them can be helpful, but some of them twist the interpretation to the point where they claim that the Bible means the opposite of what it says. In spite of their allegorizing and omissions, none of these translations can remove from the Book the supernatural events it describes, the prophecies it foretells, or the mysteries it spells out for us. Beware of the person —no matter how prominent he may be in religious circles—who tries to explain away the supernatural events as figures of speech or distorts its clear language into something more acceptable to so-called enlightened minds.

God is a Spirit. He is supernatural. We human beings are neither self-created nor the results of some cosmic accident. Just as faith is beyond logic, eternity and infinity are beyond the finite brain-power of man.

When one accepts the Bible as God's Word, he enters into an entirely new way of life. It is a way that raises doubts, asks questions, furnishes answers, and outlines a guide for decision and action. As new obstacles arise, new avenues of exploration are thrown open. Above all, it is a way that encourages a man to grow, to establish new resources of life; enlightens the eyes of his soul and calms the fears that beset him.

6

God Makes a Lot
of Promises

My experience with the Bible as a program for life— after accepting its truth and committing myself to it— can be summed up rather simply: I want to know, I want to do, I want to tell, I want to enjoy.

I want to know everything about the Bible. I want to understand its message and find clear answers to all my questions. Because I believe that the Bible is God's way of speaking to man, I want to learn what He has to say to me.

This does not come easy. It takes time, thought, and, most of all, some supernatural help. It also takes the realization that there are some things I am not supposed to know but must grow into. J. C. Penney understood this when he said, "I am convinced that the kind of faith that men need does not come by casual acceptance of a standard of conduct, important as that is. Rather, it is an experience into which we grow. Men must learn to pray, to look to God for inspiration and guidance."

A man's spiritual growth, like his physical growth,

happens slowly, by degrees, no matter how much desire or commitment he may have. In my eagerness I wanted to take giant steps, yet I had to learn to be careful in trying to develop my understanding of God's Word. Sometimes, if I am careless, I think I have found all of the revealed truth on a certain subject, only to discover later that I did not allow myself enough time to understand it. I also had to accept the bitter experience of learning some things through my mistakes.

Fortunately, if we recognize our handicaps and ask for help, God will offer us wisdom—His wisdom—in understanding what we need to know. We can count on guidance from the Holy Spirit, for God has made that promise. The person who is not willing to commit himself may dismiss this promise as foolishness, and the man who takes pride in his intellectual abilities may scoff at the concept of supernatural help, but I have experienced this guidance, and have observed many other people who experienced it, and I know it is true. I know, too, that even the most alert mind is helpless to understand the Bible without divine guidance. We must become as little children if we are to receive the fullness of the Word.

I know a man who had great difficulty in realizing the meaning of the Bible, and his problem was evident in other areas of his life as well. Although he grew up in a religious family, he did not commit himself to God until an experience at college caused him to study the Bible and devote a good deal of his time to religious work. During that time, he graduated and went into his father's business, but at first he worked neither wholeheartedly nor with a dedicated spirit. Recently he told me that a wonderful change had come into his life as a result of studying the Bible and praying for understanding. With God's help he began to realize that he resented being a junior member in his father's business and had therefore sought personal satisfaction from his religious activities. In other words, his pride—even though it stemmed from a commendable activity— became a stumbling block in his life. It made him personally distraught, miserable in his work, and frustrated in his effort to have a dependent relationship with God. When he became as a little child and sought help, God spoke to him through the words of the Bible, and showed him that personal pride was the source of his troubles. Once this man understood, he began to straighten himself out. Today he is a dynamic, effective person in both his business and religious life.

My acceptance of the Bible's truth has changed my attitudes, my desires, my interests. Not only do I want to know, but I want to do the things God tells me to do. By emphasizing the positive rather than the negative aspect of this feeling, I do not mean that I am no longer tempted to do things that I know to be wrong, or that I always do only the things I know to be right. As Paul wrote; ". . . the good that I would I do not: but the evil which I would not, that I do" (ROMANS 7:19, KJV), and that conflict exists to some degree in every human being. The difference is that now I want to do the things the Bible teaches me, even though I fall down from time to time. Certainly there are things I must not do, but I am not so much concerned about the prohibitions in my life. I feel that if I truly desire to do the right things, then the wrong things will take care of themselves.

I think it is only natural for a person who has discovered the truth to want other people to know about it, and this is the way I feel about the Good News of the Bible. Of course I run the risk of making myself obnoxious in talking about it, and some people are resentful when I try to tell them something that makes no sense to them.

Although I have made a real effort to talk about the Bible in ways that will attract rather than offend, I have had to accept the fact that no human being can explain the Bible to others unless they too desire to learn something about it, begin to ask questions, and seek the help of God's Holy Spirit. As a believer, I can make myself available and helpful to inquirers, just as other believers were helpful to me when I sought the truth, but any real acceptance of truth on their part is something between them and God.

People of every tribe and nation have always had a deepseated desire to understand how they were created and what is the purpose of life. Some people have built a thick shell around themselves, and this desire has been stifled, but it is still there and its suppression often causes serious psychological complications. Those people probably would not want to hear what I have to say. The road to understanding, in my opinion, is a supernatural one, available to all who honestly seek it, and I can be of some help to those seekers by telling them the Good News.

There are great promises in God's Word, and my commitment has made me eager to enjoy them. Understanding, serenity, the ability to overcome worry, the unburdening of guilt, the relaxation of tensions—these are some of the good things the Bible promises to believers.

Prayer, a subject in itself, is one of the most wonderful things to learn, and the man who is a believer can benefit from its power. An ability to accept the love of God and, in turn, to show love to others is another marvelous development that takes place in the believer. He is also assured of a future under the protection and guidance of the all-powerful Father. Yes, I want to enjoy all these wonderful things!

True, not every believer enjoys all these fine promises —in fact, it has been said that some people have just enough religion to make themselves miserable—but they are the people who have accepted the truth of the Bible on someone else's say-so and have not really found out for themselves what it can mean. They have only nibbled at the truth instead of making a full meal of it; they have no idea of the wonderful things that are theirs for the taking—without money and without price, as Isaiah says.

I speak from experience, my own tested experience, when I say that commitment to God's Word gives real meaning and purpose to life. It makes the days full and wonderful, it overcomes sorrows and problems, and it leads on to still greater expectations in the future. This is an experience I can demonstrate, just as I can demonstrate the things I have learned in business.

7

Learning on the Highest Level

---

*A person looking at a finished product might be mys-*tified by the way it was put together. If he had a chance to walk through a modern manufacturing plant —to see all the materials, the machines, the operators— he would probably become more confused.

The various parts of most manufactured products are made separately, on different machines, by different operators, and some of the hundreds of steps in the process would seem totally unrelated and even unnecessary to the casual viewer. It takes a production manager to appreciate that great skill is necessary in the performance of each specialized job, and that each job is essential to the finished article, and a man doesn't become a production manager simply by taking a guided tour through a factory. He has to put years of study and experience into learning each separate process.

A consumer does not have to be an experienced production man in order to appreciate a finished product. He buys something because it appears to be beautifully matched in all its parts, and if he has confidence in the manufacturer he assumes that each part was properly made.

Analogies are never perfect illustrations when applied to another field, but they do help to illuminate some similarities and some differences. It is not necessary for a consumer to experience the satisfaction of seeing all the parts of a pair of shoes fitted together in exactly the right way. But the Bible is a different matter. Some people "buy" the Bible on the basis of their faith in God, without ever trying to explore its mysteries. They may read it through once and then put it aside as something incomprehensible. Instead of studying how the many elements of the Book fit together, each portion helping to clarify another portion, they are more inclined to accept the interpretations of other people, especially those interpretations that seem to make sense to their human, finite minds.

The first difficulty with that approach is that many so-called interpreters of the Bible do not really accept its truth and they tend to tear it apart instead of letting the Spirit of God enlighten their hearts and minds. The second difficulty is that a "sensible" approach does not work when we are dealing with things beyond the range of our senses. When we study the Bible, we are dealing with supernatural ideas, and we will not get far if we depend upon explanations that seem logical to us. Here is where faith must enter in.

A man who buys a suit may think it is foolish for a manufacturer to increase the cost by putting many hand-sewn stitches in the inner lining of the lapels. He may think it more logical to eliminate the extra stitches and reduce the price. But any experienced tailor knows the value of those stitches in the appearance, fit, and wearability of the suit.

A lot of people would just as soon eliminate some parts of the Bible because they can't make any sense out of them. But I am convinced that each part is needed, and my experience has taught me that any apparent difficulty lies in me and not the Bible. I understand many parts now that once seemed puzzling to me, and as I go through life I am sure that God will reveal truths to me that I do not see today. I could not even outline the many things I have already learned about the nature of God, the nature of man, man's present state and his relation to God, the life of faith, and the prophecies of the things to come. Yet my knowledge is far from complete.

You may not agree with my views. You may think they are neither sensible, Scriptural, or even adequate —but I do not presume to tell you what you should believe. I can declare only what I believe God has taught me from the Bible. I cannot be dogmatic about the things I have learned, and I urge the reader to search them out for himself. Don't take my word for them—or the word of any other human being. Check the things I say, check what others say, and study the Bible to find out whether they are true.

8

God—
and the Man He Made

The difference between the nature of God and the nature of man is vast, so vast that it is often beyond the grasp of our minds. We human beings find it hard enough to understand ourselves, and when we try to comprehend God's extraordinary nature we can easily get lost. If we try to explore this great difference by using our own minds and our own words, we will end up by knowing less about ourselves and nothing about God. Only God's Word, the Bible, can teach us the truth about His nature and ours.

I do not know all there is to know about God and man, but the Bible has taught me that they are as different as the potter and the clay described in the Book of Jeremiah. I know that God is a Spirit and we who worship Him must worship Him in spirit and in truth, but this statement requires a great deal of thought before it can be understood. A spirit is invisible, without form or substance as I have come to understand form and substance. I cannot see it, touch it, hear it, taste it, or smell it. I can become aware of its presence only through something else—perhaps a "sixth" sense.

People define the word "spirit" in many different ways. When we use it to describe a man's state of mind, we say that he is in "good spirits." In the business world we speak of the "spirit of the organization"—the enthusiasm and loyalty of its members—and we try to build a "team spirit"—high morale, dedication to the job, and zeal to get results. We sometimes say that a man "has spirit" when we want to describe an individual characteristic. But God as a Spirit is something far beyond any of these applications of the word.

God is holy, perfect in all His attributes. Because He is holy, everything He says, does, or becomes must therefore be holy. This is true even of those things in the Bible which may not seem proper or right to us—if God through the Bible says they are right, then there can be no further questions about them. Every now and then someone will ask why God permits wars or any form of human suffering, or why He says this or that in His Word. Are we, the clay, to say to the Potter that He is wrong and we are right?

Because God is holy, He is also just. This too is hard for us to understand when all around us we see the prosperity of many people who have no faith in God, and the misfortune and tragedy in the lives of many believers. Sometimes apparent prosperity and success are only a hollow shell, and we must remember that we usually do not know all the facts involved in the lives of other people. Sometimes, too, an apparent misfortune can turn out to be a great benefit—I have found this to be true in my own observation, and I often remind myself of it by quoting the businessman's cliche, "If someone hands you a lemon, make lemonade out of it." God is a just God, and we can count on that.

I know that God is loving, and He loves us in spite of our lack of merit, our shortcomings, our disobedience, and our indifference. Love is an amazing emotion, even though we do not fully understand it in any of its phases, and God is the essence of it. It is wonderful to be loved and to be able to love others, but we can only truly love others when we have accepted the love of God in our hearts. We can get a faint glimpse of the power of this emotion when we realize that the ultimate test of love is the willingness to lay down one's life for a loved one. Not many of us could stand up to that test. God did.

I know from God's own Word that He is merciful. He knows that in my human weakness and helplessness I create many of my own problems, but He is kind and forgiving. From His infinitely high position, God cares about each one of us, not because we deserve it but because He is gracious. We will never understand His graciousness in even the smallest way until we become deeply conscious of our wrongdoings and our needs.

When or why God created our world, I do not know, nor do I believe that anyone else really knows. I believe the Bible when it tells me that this world was partially destroyed after its original creation and that a new creation followed that cataclysmic shakeup. That is what the Book of Genesis means when it says the "earth *had become* waste and void."

In this new creation God made more than the physical world; He also created man, a creature of a higher order than plants and animals. Despite many contrary theories—and the scientists admit that they are only theories—I am convinced that man was specially created by God and is entirely different from any other form of life.

Man has been given a small measure of knowledge and wisdom, and he will receive more as he asks for it, but God has all knowledge and wisdom. He has always existed, and as the Creator of the universe He knows all the laws and principles of every field of science, including the few that man has discovered and the many he has not yet imagined. As the Creator of earth and man, God knows all about physiology, psychology, sociology, economics, business, mathematics, and every other branch of learning. Man, through his puny efforts, has learned a little and sometimes thinks he has accomplished a lot, but how small is his knowledge compared to all God knows!

Through His own Word in the Bible we are taught that God is the Creator of energy—the enormous energy of the suns, the forces that move the planets, and the energy of life itself. While some people dispute this truth, no one has yet come up with a halfway sensible "natural" explanation of the origin of energy. In my own attempt at trying to understand the infinite, I find much more sense in the concept of a supernatural Power who not only created the universe but applied the energy to keep it going.

God put a lot of laws into motion when He created

the universe, but He has the power to change them because He is the omnipotent Creator of everything. He can control men or let them alone, He can cause things to happen through the laws He created, or He can make things happen independently of them.

The enormity of God's power is beyond us. We think of power in terms of brilliant men in positions of authority, the might of military machines, the strength of huge organizations, or the forces of electricity, explosives, wind, or water. These are nothing compared to the power of God.

A human being finds it hard to understand that God limits His power at times. For instance, God created man with a free will, which means that man can make decisions about the way he is going to live. God knows what decisions a man is going to make—and often they will be the wrong ones—but He does not use His power to change the man's mind because that would interfere with his free will. God has urged us in His Word to choose goodness and life, but He permits us to choose evil and death.

It is true that the Bible speaks of God changing His mind on some occasions, but that is only what seems to happen in the eyes of men. The nature of God never changes, because a perfect God must always be perfect. In His perfect foresight, He knows all of the future; and since it is directed according to His purpose and will, there is really no need for Him to change. His infinite powers of love and mercy, combined with His perfect justice, allow Him plenty of room to deal with mankind. If we sometimes think God has changed, it is because He must reveal Himself to us in a changing way. Just as the Bible is made up of a series of developing relationships and revelations, God must reveal Himself gradually to man because that is the only way a human mind will ever comprehend Him.

God is everywhere, and perhaps this is one of the most complicated aspects of His nature. How can this Spirit we call God be in all places throughout the universe—and at the same time? How can I know that He will always be right here when I need to reach out and feel His presence? David answers, in effect (PSALM 139): "I cannot escape from the presence of God, even if I would. Whether it is heaven or hades, darkness or light, God is there. Even if I take the wings of the morning and dwell in the uttermost parts of the sea; even there shall Thy hand lead me, and Thy right hand hold me." And one of the Proverbs tells us that "The eyes of the Lord are in every place, beholding the evil and the good" (15:3, KJV).

A man who once led a wild life and then changed his ways was asked by a friend whether he was ever tempted to revert to his former life, especially when he was alone. His answer defined his understanding of the ever-present God: "But, you see, I am never alone." We need to be aware of this truth always. God knows our innermost thoughts as well as our actions, and we can never pretend with Him.

Far from being uncomfortable, this constant presence is a wonderful thing. It means we can always be in touch with Someone who knows us, who understands our problems, and who will listen sympathetically when we pour out our hearts. It means we can always look to Someone for understanding, wisdom, strength, and love.

Man has a great need for contact with this presence, and when he is unable to reach out for it his life can become seriously disturbed. One of the matters of concern today in a business organization is the mental health of its executives, for an executive with mental problems cannot perform his functions properly or act as a leader for others. This concern has even caused some companies to employ psychiatrists as consultants for their executives. Psychiatrists are being asked for solutions to many other kinds of human problems, and psychoanalysis, a special field of psychiatry, is becoming almost a vogue in some of our larger cities.

I am sure that some troubled individuals may need psychiatric, and perhaps even psychoanalytical help for the illnesses that afflict them; in some cases people may require drugs or shock treatment. But too many people are trying to substitute sessions with an analyst for a relationship with God, and they will never find what they are seeking. The most effective kind of therapy for man is a close contact with his Creator which permits him to unburden his heart. And this is constantly available to us in the omnipresence of God.

When we read about God in the Bible, we find that He is called by different names, some of them singular, some of them plural. These names express different features of God because He reveals Himself to us in many ways, but there is only one God. John the Apostle makes it clear that Jesus is the incarnation of God—

God taking on the form of man—but Jesus is God Himself and has always existed. While the Holy Spirit is another manifestation of God, He is still God Himself. Therefore when we speak of God the Father, God the Son, and God the Holy Spirit, we speak of the one God, the Creator, the omnipotent, omnipresent, omniscient Spirit. These distinctions are made clear in the Bible.

Man can also learn the truth about himself from the Bible. He can discover that the first man was created an innocent being, without the knowledge of evil. Because a perfect God would not create something that was imperfect, man was created a perfect physiological and psychological organism. He was never meant to be an automaton and was given the right to make his own choices as a free moral agent.

Placed in a perfect environment, man was given a perfect wife so that he could have companionship and could exercise the physiological function of procreation. He was created a mortal being, which means that he was to reproduce himself in his offspring even though he himself would die a physical death. He was, in fact, commanded to produce children, and all his descendants are part of his original creation. Neither you, nor I, nor anyone else can claim that our physical existence came about through a separate act of God, for we are all natural results of the creation of the original man.

Although man was given free will, he was not left without instructions about the wise choices in life. God Himself explained the facts of life to the original man, pointing out how he could obtain eternal life and how he could gain the knowledge of good and evil. At first, man was not forbidden to seek to make himself eternal, but God explained that he was not, on pain of death, to seek the knowledge of good and evil. In no uncertain terms man was warned, and then he was given the freedom to make up his own mind.

And what did man do? He deliberately disobeyed and did exactly what his Creator had forbidden him to do. He chose death when he could have chosen life.

Anyone with business experience can look back on his mistakes and bad choices, for they are part of his present and his future. It isn't often that we deliberately do something we know to be wrong, but sometimes it happens, and then the law of compensation goes into effect. We must suffer the consequences of our mistakes and we can blame no one but ourselves.

The first man knew the penalty for doing what was forbidden; nevertheless he did it. Because he had been warned, he could not hide from his disobedience—and that of his companion—as he tried to hide from God, and his penalty was the inevitable consequence of his act.

When man accepted God's curse and began to carry its burden, his life changed. An exile from the perfect environment he had known, he was condemned to hard labor, trouble, and pain. No longer could he, on his own, hope to find eternal life, for God had closed the way to it—but he would find death.

Although his surroundings changed, man's physical nature remained the same. He was still to reproduce himself in his children and in his children's children.

These children, who would be physical extensions of the original man, would inherit the willful disobedience of his nature, and they too would share his condemnation to toil, trouble, pain, and death. There was to be only one exception.

We who were born so many years later are included in that original man's original sin. Physically, we were born in sin, and if we are to understand ourselves at all we must first understand that we are basically evil. True, mankind has an inclination to do good, but not the nature to be good.

A great many people resent this truth because they cannot bear to think of themselves as being essentially evil. When they think of evil, they think in terms of criminals, scoundrels, and hardhearted people. What about all those people who try to live clean, moral lives? What about those who obviously have integrity, a sense of fair play, and a kindly feeling toward others? Are they evil? We are all evil, although we do not express our evil nature in the same ways. Some of us, through our philosophy or our fear of law or public opinion, have been able to discipline our inherited evil nature—or at least the outward expression of it. The very process of becoming civilized means that a man must train himself to live decently with other members of society, and this training involves the subjection of his evil nature. When training is absent or insufficient, man's evil nature runs rampant, and it is very easy to point a finger at such examples. On the other hand, no one seriously claims to be perfect, no matter how well he behaves, and that is because no amount of discipline can completely subdue the evil within us.

A business associate of mine is a very able man who knows his job, works hard, has a strong personality, and high integrity. He also has a blind spot. If the volume of business in his division is not what it should be, he always thinks the problem comes from outside his area of responsibility. He simply does not want to face the fact that his own efforts may not be exactly right. And so it is with many of us. We do not like to face unpleasant facts about ourselves, and we build up our blind spots with alibis and rationalizations.

We don't feel comfortable when we have to admit that we must constantly suppress our evil desires and thoughts. How much pleasanter it is to show ourselves to the public as people of decency, culture, and fairness! We do not want to climb up on a pedestal, but neither do we want to be classified with lawbreakers and dissolute people.

Admitting that our inner nature is basically evil does not mean that we have to classify ourselves with criminals. It means that we have come closer to understanding what the Bible means when it says that every imagination of the thoughts of man's heart "are only evil continually" (GENESIS 6:5). Our well-developed blind spots keep us from seeing our inner evil, but it is there.

The Bible described man's nature a long time ago, and some people wonder whether the description is still valid. They point to the progress of world civilization and imply that mankind is now on a much higher plane of existence. After all, man has gained a great deal of knowledge during the past six thousand years—particularly during the past fifty years when the advances in scientific knowledge have been staggering. Today we can transport ourselves to almost any point in the world within a matter of hours; we can speak to anyone, anywhere, at any time; we can see pictures of things that are happening thousands of miles away; we can produce more food with less labor, and we live longer, more active lives with the aid of new medical discoveries; we have made amusements, entertainment, and education available to almost everyone; we are erecting buildings, laying down superhighways, and creating new materials out of air, water, and other basic resources.

Has man changed as much as his environment? Is there more justice in the world? Have we eliminated war? Do people love each other more? Have politicians become more honest? Have our prisons been emptied? Have our mental hospitals gone out of business for lack of patients? Have our businessmen cleaned up their ethics? Do women, or men, no longer need protection on city streets at night? Have drunkenness, prostitution, and sodomy disappeared? Do our church members live at peace with each other? Have gossip, jealousy, envy, lust, and a thousand other "oldtime" sins vanished?

We all know the answers. Man, in spite of his veneer of civilization and scientific knowledge, is the same as ever. He has the same inherently evil nature and the same inclination to do good. This marvelous inclination, though not fully developed, leaves its marks in the world, and I do not wish to minimize it. Through the efforts of many self-sacrificing people, the sick are being helped and more hospitals are being built; education is being made available to many more people; helping hands are being extended to many of the poor and unfortunate, and many orphaned and abandoned children are being cared for; in most places law and order are being preserved. A few cynics may say that there are some dubious motives behind all the good deeds that are done, but I prefer to rejoice whenever man's inclination tries to overcome his nature. His good deeds need plenty of encouragement.

When we can accept the Bible's truth about God and man, we can begin to understand why there was a vast separation between them. Permanent as it seemed, God intended to bring man back into the warmth of His love. How could it be done? Certainly not through man, helpless and disobedient as he was. Could God put aside His condemnation of Adam? That would make of God a liar because He had warned Adam of the penalty for disobedience. It would make of Satan a truth-teller because the evil spirit had told Adam that God was not speaking the truth when He warned of punishment. How was perfect God in His perfect love to deal in perfect justice with imperfect, willful man? That was a dilemma only God could resolve.

9

Only God Could Have Done It!

---

*The evil in our human nature makes us slow to un-*derstand ourselves. We know we are guilty of wrong-doing and evil desires, so we try to overcome it with good works or we seek escape in hard work, pleasure, or alcohol. When our guilt becomes too painful we compare ourselves with other people and rationalize ourselves into a better mood. We always plan to do better, to avoid temptations, and to live decently, so no one can say we aren't trying.

Still, there is that nagging thought in the back of our minds—"Someday these things will catch up with me! Someday I'm going to be punished for the things I should do and don't—and for the things I shouldn't do and do." If we should get sick, or lose something, or suffer a great misfortune, we will be getting what we deserve—so we feel on the inside.

We simply can't be honest with ourselves and admit that we do not have the inherent ability to live as we should. Adam had the same trouble. He could not undo the evil choice he had made. He could not expiate his disobedience against God by doing good works or by living a perfect life because his evil nature prevented it.

So what was Adam to do? Forget about the whole thing? Eat, drink, and be merry, and tomorrow it might go away? Or should he escape from the voice of his guilty conscience or shut up the ears of his heart? Maybe he could do penance by lending a helping hand to other people. It wouldn't change his evil nature, but it might make him feel better.

The reconciliation between God and man was something man could do nothing about, for it was to come through a process that was independent of his actions. Some people call it "conversion," or "salvation," or "becoming a believer." Call it what you will, it fulfilled the purpose of God and offered the perfect solution to the dilemma of God's justice and love, and man's disobedience.

Mankind was freed from condemnation when God took upon Himself the punishment for the crime. He did this by creating a Second Man, a new Adam, who did not have an inherently evil nature. Jesus Christ is the one exception, the only Man who did not inherit Adam's sinful nature, because He was neither a part of the physical creation of the first man nor his natural descendant. Jesus Christ was a new creation, God taking the form of man, and we human beings can claim no physical kinship with Him.

We are descendants of Adam, but Christ is not. When the Second Man was brought into being, the power of the most high God miraculously overshadowed a virgin and a Babe was conceived, a new creation without a human father. Equally man and equally God, Jesus became subject to man's environment. Having always existed in the spirit, He took on the earthly body of flesh so that God's purpose might be fulfilled. The first man is natural—of the earth; the Second Man is spiritual—the Lord Himself from heaven.

The New Man was perfect and He obeyed God even though He was tempted as we are. He lived a human life without an evil thought, without a single disobedient act, and with love and kindness for His fellow men. Surely such a Person deserved the best of everything in this life—as well as in the life to come—yet that was not the purpose of His coming. He came to offer His perfect human life in the place of the first man—and thus to pay the penalty of death for man's evil.

Jesus Christ gave up His life voluntarily. This Man who was under no curse submitted to the power of evil, was degraded, spat upon, nailed to a cross, ridiculed, shamed, and killed. It could have been different. Jesus in His divine power could have avoided the cross. Had He used His godly power in different ways, men would have extolled Him instead of killing Him. But that would have been disobedient, too, and Jesus was not like Adam. He fulfilled God's purpose by expiating the curse placed upon Adam and opened up a pathway for God's holy power and love to work in the world.

Through the crucifixion man was able to return to the bliss he had known in paradise, but that did not cover the full purpose of God. In his original environment man had been told of the opportunity for eternal life, and that was still withheld from him through the consequences of Adam's sin. Jesus Christ, the God-Man, had indeed expiated the disobedience of mankind, but in submitting Himself to the power of evil He had been killed. Man was free to make a new choice, but was there any choice left? Had God destroyed the possibility of eternal life by allowing Himself to be destroyed by evil?

From a human standpoint, it seemed that Jesus had been destroyed, and the future seemed hopeless. A Man of promise had been cut down at a young age and He had left no written instructions to His followers, those frightened men of little influence and ability. Not even an organization remained to carry on His philosophy and teachings. The leaders of world government in Rome had not even heard about the frustrated movement in Palestine and they could go about their affairs without worrying about what was happening in that faraway province.

The power of evil holds sway in this world, but it has limitations. It took the perfect Life that was offered up, abused it, trampled it to the full extent of its power, but it could not destroy the divine element in it. This failure was announced to the world through an event so strange that few people believed it at the time it happened—and many people doubt it today. Jesus Christ —crucified, dead, and placed in a tomb for three days —came back to life. He had left the tomb and was moving about freely in new strength and power. Impossible! From a human or scientific standpoint, yes, and many people shrugged it off, pitying the poor fools who believed such nonsense. Still the reports continued, in spite of disbelief, and there were those who said they saw Him, talked with Him, touched Him.

From a scattered, frightened, disillusioned group of followers of the human Jesus came forth people with bold convictions who felt a new power within themselves. They began to understand the full purpose of God as they had not understood it before, and no amount of disbelief or resistance could shake their conviction. No dreams, no fairy tales, no pep talks could have produced the results they achieved.

From my many years of experience as a leader of a business organization consisting of many thousands of people, I know something about what it takes to get people to put forth their best efforts in the most effective way. Underlying many other important factors must be a real conviction on the part of people that they are being asked to do something worthwhile, something right for them, something based on truth. Anyone who tries to get people to go into something with their whole hearts, but without conviction, will not get results.

People must be dedicated to their jobs in order to be successful, and no amount of ability or personality can overcome a lack of dedication. As I think of individuals who have missed a certain measure of success because they were not dedicated to their work, I can attribute it to several reasons. Sometimes it came from their selfish desire to exalt themselves instead of giving precedence to the job to be done. Some put pleasure before duty and some were frustrated by problems with their families or associates. One of the ablest men I know missed a full measure of success in his business because every time he had to make a decision he gave first consideration to his personal status and how the decision would affect it. Dedication means that we must forget ourselves and give first consideration to the requirements of the job to be done. This is quite well expressed in the old saying, "If a man will take care of his business first, his business will take care of him."

The followers of Jesus were able to throw themselves completely into bringing His message to the world because they were dedicated men. Their conviction came suddenly when they saw Jesus alive after He had been crucified and buried, and they were able to accomplish great things because their eyes were open to the full meaning of God's purpose. Once aware of its truth, its worthiness, and its rightness for them, they began to gain the inner security that is essential to dedication.

The resurrection of Jesus Christ means that the power of God overcame the power of evil, that life overcame death, that mankind was again offered the opportunity to gain eternal life with its new powers and new understanding. Unlike the life in the flesh which is subject to corruption and limited in its existence, understanding, and power, this new life is incorruptible and unlimited.

When Jesus came alive after His death on the cross, He had a new kind of body. His appearance was the same, because His friends knew Him when they saw Him. They could touch Him, walk with Him, see the wounds in His flesh, but there was no blood in His new body and He could change His appearance, transport

Himself from place to place in an instant, go through closed doors, and even disappear.

Jesus has a spiritual, an incorruptible body. I am speaking of Him now in the present tense because He has overcome death and His new body has unlimited existence and power. He lives today, using His power to move from one place to another, to change His appearance as He sees fit, or not to appear at all. Whether or not we see Him, He is always present.

Reconciliation is a long word with many overtones to its meaning, but it is important for us to try to understand it. Through Jesus Christ, God has opened up a channel by which man can come to Him once again, in a way that satisfies both His perfect love and perfect justice. The power of evil will try to stop men from understanding this revelation, and we must not fall into the trap of relying upon our own intellect to guide us. Reconciliation is something we must learn from God, and we have God's own Word to teach us. It can tell us how we can come to God and receive the opportunity to choose eternal life, and it can tell us in detail about the new birth we will experience if we make that choice.

The New
Spiritual Embryo

One of the best-known stories in the Bible describes a farmer sowing his seed. We can imagine the farmer striding along under the bright sun, reaching rhythmically into the sack slung over his shoulder for handfuls of seed and casting the grains from his experienced fingers so that they scatter over the ground.

Not all the seed that falls to the ground will yield crops for the farmer. Some of it is quickly snatched up by birds only seconds after it is thrown; a certain amount drops along the road or in the pathway where it is trampled before it has a chance to germinate; and some of it lands among rocky patches in the soil where it cannot take root and is soon choked by the weeds that seem to thrive there. The seed that falls onto good soil will grow up into healthy stalks of grain that will make the farmer feel his toil has been worthwhile. Sometimes as many as one hundred kernels of grain will come from one seed that fell among nourishing soil.

The Bible often teaches us by illustration, and when

we read the Parable of the Sower we are really learning about the process by which God creates new spiritual beings within men. The seed in this story is the Word of God, as given us in the Bible; and as this Word is sown in the heart of the physical human being, it becomes the nucleus for the spiritual life that can come to life in him.

The birth and maturation of this spiritual being is similar in some ways to the physiological birth and maturation of the human being. When the seed of man is planted in the woman, some of it germinates and grows into another human being—not, of course, a new creation, but a continuation of the original creation.

Jesus Christ, the Second Man, is a spiritual being, and His seed, the Word of God, is sown in the hearts of men. Under suitable conditions it germinates and grows there, but not all spiritual beings develop in identical ways. Just as seeds of grain will produce varying degrees of fruitfulness in the stalks, some of the spiritual beings will be more useful than others.

Every father and mother must have experienced an awesome wonder at the amazing events of conception, gestation, and birth. It is still the mystery of mysteries, even though it has happened billions of times in the history of the human race, and the more we try to simplify our explanation of it, the more we discover its marvelous complexity.

A human being cannot be conceived unless the seed of the man is good and the season and conditions of the woman are favorable. In this remarkable way it is similar to the birth of a new spiritual being. The human heart is the ground for the spiritual seed—the mother, if we are to carry the analogy further—and it must be in a receptive condition when the Word of God is sown if it is to conceive new life. A heart that is in a receptive condition is one that is willing to listen to the Word. It is like the good soil that receives the scattered seed. Nothing will grow in the stony-hearted man who refuses to let his inner soul contemplate any idea of the spiritual nature, for he is like the roadway in the parable. Conception by rape does not occur in the spiritual realm, and in this sense the two birth processes differ.

A receptive heart is also convicted of its need. It knows of man's guilt and realizes that he is helpless to cope with life's problems by himself. A heart is convicted when the Spirit of God takes hold of it, warms it, opens it up, and prepares it to receive the Word, and it is quite possible that this happens to each human heart, periodically, in ways we do not understand. (We can find evidence of rhythms and cycles everywhere in God's created universe.)

Whatever the process and however it comes about, under proper conditions and at the right times the Word of God comes to life in the heart of a human being and a spiritual conception takes place. It may seem presumptuous to say that these new spiritual beings are the same as Jesus Christ in a spiritual sense, but this is what the Bible teaches us. By a spiritual process of love, Jesus Christ reproduces Himself in new conceptions within human hearts, and these new beings are spiritually one with Him. They are extensions of the Second Man, in His image, just as we are now physical extensions of the first physical man.

After conception, there is a period of gestation in the

spiritual process, as there is in the physical, but some of our translations of the New Testament do not make this clear. Gestation in the spiritual sense is much longer. I believe that it lasts as long as the human being lives on this earth and that the new spiritual being is fully born —after the gestation period—when the flesh dies. As the grain of wheat dies that a new life may be born, so the flesh dies that a new spiritual existence can come into full being. In a letter to the Corinthians (1, 15:36), Paul explains that the seed is not "quickened," or brought to full life, until it dies—and we know that in the death of Jesus' fleshly body, His new spiritual body was brought to life. That same kind of spiritual body will come about in believers when their fleshly bodies die.

The Word of God is powerful and contains within it the principle of new life. It is seed sown throughout the world in the hearts of men but, like the seed in the parable, some of it falls in stony places or on the roadway itself where it is choked by worldly activities. Only a portion of it finds fertile ground where it can germinate, and the new spiritual embryos thus conceived will grow into a full spiritual existence like that of Jesus Christ in His resurrected life.

While we are here on earth, the new life within us is slowly being shaped and perfected, but the process is far from peaceful. The new seed, being spiritual, comes into conflict with the flesh that contains it and begins to struggle against it, much as the human embryo struggles in the womb. This struggle ends with the death of the flesh and the final perfect emergence of the spiritual being.

Spiritual embryos are entirely different from human embryos in their relationship to each other. Human embryos are separated from each other, each in its own womb. The world itself might be considered one great womb containing countless spiritual embryos, struggling, suffering, growing in darkness, trying to come into the light of the spiritual life through birth. All are part of the body of Christ.

How wonderful it is to realize that every human being, even though sharing in the curse of the first man, can become the home of a new spiritually created being! It means that mankind is the soil in which God's Word can come into new existence. Without that Word, that spiritual seed, mankind is nothing more than the soil of the earth, a habitation for weeds and crawling things. By receiving the Word, man receives the love of Christ Himself, and the human act of love is only a weak comparison to such ecstasy.

The man who accepts the truth of God's Word, and through it the love of Christ, is learning the full meaning of life and he is no longer the same. How does such a person live? How does he behave? Does he follow a new set of rules and regulations, giving up past pleasures and desires? Does he have any freedom of action?

When a man's fleshly body harbors a new spiritual being, he does not need any set of rules, nor must he conform to the dictates of any person or council. The spiritual nature within him is like the nature of Christ: it is inherently good and delights in the things that are good. Because it naturally avoids evil, it is not led astray by the rotten things that look good on the surface.

The struggle between his spiritual nature and his human nature confronts the believer with a new problem. He must try to subdue the evil desires of the flesh and allow his spiritual nature full sway in his life. The greater his achievement in this effort, the greater will be his joy. This is not done through sacrifice or giving up past pleasures; on the contrary, the believer finds that his desires have changed and the old ways have lost their ability to please—if they ever really had it. When a man truly finds pleasure in good things, he finds many new avenues of joy and excitement.

It is true that some believers have a sad, sacrificial attitude toward their lives, as if they have given up something valuable. Perhaps the guilt of their past behavior weighs heavily upon them, or they may have been taught that sadness and sacrifice were essential to spiritual rebirth—whatever the reason, their attitude is an indication of their spiritual immaturity.

Man's spiritual development is similar to his physical development in that the embryo must grow, and its growth depends upon nourishment, exercise, and instruction. If the spirit within him cannot mature, a man is helpless against the evil desires of his flesh and will never approach the state of happiness God makes available to him.

Like milk for the newborn babe, God's Word is the essential food for the spiritual entity. In ways that we do not understand, the Bible nourishes the spiritual person, enabling it to grow, gain strength, and persist in its struggle against the flesh. Just as physical food works differently in different people, spiritual nourishment will not produce the same rate of growth in all believers. Sound growth is a slow process, hard to measure, but those who feed regularly on God's Word will surely grow, and we must not neglect our essential food simply because we cannot mark off the inches on our spiritual growth.

Man-made things tend to wear out as they are used —machinery in a manufacturing plant, gadgets in the home—but this is not the case with our bodies. A healthy body needs plenty of exercise to develop its muscles and keep all its parts functioning effectively. Without good exercise we deteriorate, and the same thing is true of our spiritual muscles and fibers.

When it is not hampered by the flesh, the spiritual nature seeks to exercise the talents God has given it. Not all spiritual entities have the same talents, and it is important for the believer to recognize this diversity of gifts. The wrong kind of exercise will leave the spirit's best abilities unused, and God's gifts are not meant to be wasted.

Paul referred to this diversity in a letter to the Corinthians, explaining that people are variously gifted with the ability to speak effectively, or to interpret and teach, or to govern and administer authority, or to heal and alleviate the sick, or to handle business matters. We are all gifted in some way, but we cannot discover our peculiar talents by watching the abilities of someone else. If we can subdue our evil fleshly tendencies and follow the inclination of our spiritual nature, we can find out what it is we do well. Then it is our job to exercise that talent by giving it the opportunity to work in our lives. God is our Heavenly Father, and He watches over the activities of His children just as earthly parents supervise their children. He wants our spiritual embryos to grow into strong, well-developed spiritual persons and He will provide them with the kind of exercise that exactly suits their capabilities. When the believer is spiritually dominated, he will find plenty of opportunity to use the talents he discovers in himself.

The human body has eyes, feet, ears, arms, and other members, and the spiritual members of the body of Christ also must perform different functions with their various talents. All are needed, but the combination of abilities in each spiritual person is always unique. In the business world, we know that it is most important to try to find the best place for each individual, for no two people are exactly alike. I have known many people who have been able to recognize their best abilities, and it seems that almost automatically the doors of opportunity open before them. I have known others who, in their human zeal and eagerness, reached out too far, and in the wrong direction, and went ahead of the leading of their spiritual inclinations. Sometimes a man is so ambitious for position or money that he is not content to stay in the job that suits his talents; or, in other cases, a man may hesitate to reach for the kind of work his talent fits. Either way, a man makes his own unhappiness and ends up with the feeling of inadequacy.

I knew a man who worked very hard, but always against the grain of his abilities. He had a splendid mind, enormous energy and enthusiasm, but he was a do-it-himself type of person who simply could not delegate work to anyone else. He felt he had to do as well as his father—who was a strong, successful executive— but he did not have his father's toughmindedness or his ability to supervise the work of others. By spreading himself out too far and too thin, he never had the feeling of achievement and he wasted his best gifts. He would have been much happier and more effective doing a job that was completely under his immediate supervision.

The Bible can help us to understand ourselves, to face realities, and many a man has been able to find himself and see where he fits into the workaday world by studying this Book written so many centuries ago. When a person is willing to learn, he can change the pattern of frustration in his life, letting his past failures serve as a means of development for his spiritual nature.

Through feeding on the Word of God, and through the successes and failures of exercise, the growing spiritual being receives a certain amount of instruction, but it needs a good deal more. We do a lot of talking about education these days, and I think most of us appreciate its value in the development of the human being. Education means much more than schooling, and although the words are often used interchangeably, they are not the same. Many people who have spent years in school are never really educated, and many well-educated people have never received academic degrees or, for that matter, much formal schooling.

The most important factor in any man's education is his desire to learn, and it is difficult to create that desire. Some people have it and others do not. When a man is educated, it means that he has acquired knowledge—within the limits of his intellectual capacity—and that he understands what he has acquired. He has learned about ideas and about people, and he knows how to communicate these ideas to other people.

God has provided us with many opportunities to educate our young spiritual natures. Perhaps the most generally accepted means of spiritual instruction is to learn from people who are using their God-given talents to teach. Most of us learn by listening, and as we listen to persons who can reach us and stimulate us, we will find new vistas of knowledge opening before us. Spiritual instruction is one of the great purposes of church meetings, and it is there that our spiritual nature should be able to find much of the education it needs.

In addition to the spoken word, the spiritual nature should be brought into contact with the great mass of literature on spiritual matters. Books, periodicals, and pamphlets can broaden our spiritual horizons, clear up questions that arise in the educational process, and offer new opportunities for exercise.

When we listen to other people, when we read and study, we must be very careful to avoid getting involved with the wrong kind of instructors—and there are many. Just as human children can be led astray by the wrong teachers, so the growth of the spiritual infant can be thwarted if it does not have its Father's guidance in all its instruction. That is why the most important part of our spiritual development is prayer, our two-way communication with God. It is the channel by which God teaches us directly, and it involves both speaking and listening.

There is no short-cut to the art of prayer, nor is it a course that can be learned in any school. God is our Teacher, and His step-by-step instruction is the most vital part of our spiritual education.

11

Prayer Is Deeper Than Words

I once participated in a small group of businessmen who had been asked by a university to study and recommend the kind of academic preparation a college student would need for a career in business. After a year of investigation we all agreed that the best way the university could make students more useful to the business world was to teach them how to communicate. We felt that the most essential quality in a successful businessman was his ability to listen to someone else, to express himself clearly, to ask useful questions, to read figures as well as words, and to analyze the flow of communication available to him.

Communication is never a one-way affair, for it involves the exchange of information between two or more people. More than their understanding of the words used, communication means that these people must understand each other. When they converse, people exchange information by their current moods, by their facial expressions, by inference, by tone and quality of voice as well as by words. Communication is therefore a complicated subject requiring careful study.

So it is with prayer, by which we communicate with God. The Bible has answered my questions about prayer and has taught me its wonderful uses in the life of faith. It tells me that when we pray we are like children talking to their father, and this is important in understanding the relationship that is the foundation of prayer.

Spiritual communication is far deeper and more complicated than anything we know in the field of human communication. We can make use of some basic prayer guides to help us along the way, but the real foundation in our training must be built on practice and experience.

If we are to understand the meaning of prayer, we must first understand the concept of spiritual entities. God is a Spirit and we are flesh. How then can a human being communicate with a Spiritual Being? If the human being is only an extension of the old Adam who disobeyed God and brought God's curse upon himself and his descendants, communication is out of the question. Such a man is dead, as far as his spiritual existence is concerned. Only when God Himself has created a new spirit within the human being can real spiritual communication become possible, for then it becomes an exchange between two spiritual beings. Our bodies are as incapable of spiritual communication as the earthly soil on which we live, but the spiritual natures developing within us have the marvelous ability to form a connection with the Holy Spirit which is God.

Some people may raise an objection at this point and say that Adam and other Biblical patriarchs were still able to receive communication from God after they were under the curse. That is true, but we cannot be certain that it was truly a two-way communication. It is also possible that God created a new spiritual entity within some of those human beings because He knew from the beginning that He planned to reconcile man with His justice and love through a new race of spiritually reborn people.

Another basic principle of prayer involves our acknowledgment of God's omnipresence. Even though it is beyond our human comprehension, we must accept the truth that God as a Spirit is always available to each of His spiritual children, no matter how many may call on Him at the same time and from many different places.

If we are to learn how prayer works, we must understand its purpose. We do not pray in order to change the mind of God, or to remind Him of things we think He may have overlooked. It is not our job to give God instructions or to arouse Him to activity, as if He were asleep or busy with other matters. Many of us fall into these errors, quite unconsciously, when we approach prayer and that is one of the reasons why we fail to communicate. God knows what we need and what is best for us—far better than we do.

Since God knows so much about us, why bother to communicate with Him at all? This is a perfectly natural question, but its answer is not simple. We must always remember that while we are able to understand all we need to know about God and the way He operates, we have no business asking ,"Why?" God does not always choose to tell us His reasons for doing certain things in certain ways—and even if He were to tell us everything, it is doubtful that we could comprehend it. We should be satisfied because God is ready to reveal what He thinks we ought to know for the time being, and we can be sure that as we grow spiritually we will have a clearer understanding of many more things. We can all remember that when we were little children our parents had to answer our questions gradually, according to our ability to understand. Our spiritual natures must learn in the same way, and it is incorrect to assume that through prayer we will get the all-in-one answer to our all-in-one question.

Prayer helps us to get to know God and to identify ourselves with Him. It is the connection—the wire —that carries the electric current of prayer power. God's power cannot come into the world through the descendants of the first man because man is cut off from God by sin, but it can be transmitted through the new spiritual beings within us, these second-men through whom we can claim kinship with Christ. Prayer is not a means of telling God what to do, but a means of finding out what God wants to do. And it is so much more. We are not able to understand our spiritual needs any more than children know what is right for them, but through prayer we can learn of our needs from God Himself. We can discover the mind of God so that it can become our mind, too, and we can gain access to God's perfect knowledge so that we can be activated by its perfect power. In this way God can minister to our needs.

Some psychologists have tried to explain prayer as a

form of autosuggestion, or self-hypnosis, and it is entirely possible that the prayer exercise can, in some cases, exhibit some of these aspects. Undoubtedly, autosuggestion as used in psychological therapy may have beneficial results in training a person's emotional nature, but anyone who has experienced prayer as a relationship with God knows that it is much more than a psychological experience. Both the nonbeliever and the believer can experience autosuggestion, but only the believer can know prayer. Regardless of his sincerity, the nonbeliever can do no more than make external observations about prayer.

When we understand the meaning of prayer we can accept the fact that God's power can be brought to bear on a person who may be far away from the one who is praying. This is called intercessory prayer. It means that I can pray for someone I know in South America and instantly the power of God will have a channel through which it can enter that person's life. I can prove this only by my experience, and it has happened over and over in my life. God's power has entered my life many times through people who have prayed for me, and I know that I have been able to serve as a similar channel for His power for other people. I am at a loss to explain how these results are accomplished, but I can hardly question the truth of them. Although I can understand something of the principles of prayer, I am still mystified by the way it works. I only know that it does work and I am deeply grateful for my experiences of it.

If prayer is the simple process of opening up a channel for the perfect power of God to come into the world, why hasn't the whole world come completely under that power? Why are suffering, injustice, and evil still with us? If I can call upon God's power whenever I will, why can't I solve all my problems? Why can't I have perfect wisdom and give help to all the people who need it?

We cannot answer all these questions until we realize that our world is not in a power vacuum. When the spirit of evil entered the world through the disobedience of the first man, it took possession of the world. We do not know why the all-powerful God allowed this spirit to dominate the world, or why its domination continues, but that is what happened. If prayer were simply a matter of establishing a contact between our spiritual natures and God, perhaps we would not have any questions to ask today, but that is not the case. The power of evil is constantly seeking to prevent our spiritual natures from communicating with God and becoming a channel for His power, and often it succeeds. When we hold onto evil thoughts or habits, we cut off real prayer communication with God. The power of God, always available to man, is therefore resisted and rejected by man whenever he submits to the evil desires of his flesh—and it takes a great deal of the believer's effort to subdue his human nature.

We must also realize that prayer is an art, and most of us do not know how to use it well. Spiritually, we are only embryos, weak and imperfect. We have to grow up and gradually learn how to make use of our spiritual strength. In other words, we supply very imperfect channels through which God's power can enter and become active in the world.

Imperfect though we are, God has arranged matters so that we are the only channels for His power to enter the world, and that is why our spiritual development is so important. Prayer is a vital part of our development and we must study its art and practice its discipline with patience and determination. If we can understand the basic principles of prayer, we can begin to learn the art of praying, and then we can find out for ourselves whether it really works. The place to begin our study is the Bible.

12

Dialogue for God and Man

When Jesus was on the earth, His followers asked Him to teach them how to pray. Jesus Himself was a Man of prayer; by the many hours He spent communicating with His Father, He showed us its great importance in the spiritual life. He knew that there were many things we must learn about prayer and that we must learn them slowly.

The Bible has taught me the meaning of prayer, but that is only the first step. I have also learned from God's own Word that a man must meet certain other requirements if he is to converse with God.

Prayer requires a belief in God and a belief in prayer —or at least in the possibility of prayer. It makes no sense for a person to pray to something he rejects in principle, for if he is to receive power he must believe in the existence of that power. Our faith does not have to be great or perfect—doubts may press upon us and we may be mystified by both God and prayer—but we must have some degree of acceptance of God's love through belief in His Son.

God is our spiritual Father, and we must come to Him as children when we pray. When we were very young, we expected our parents to look after us, to feed us and protect us, and as spiritual children we can now expect that God will minister to our spiritual needs. He always does.

As children, we used to make extra demands upon our parents and we do the same thing with God in our prayers. I think we can all remember times when we asked our parents for something that was not really good for us, and they had to say "no." So must God say "no" to some of our requests, but that does not mean that He refuses to listen to some of our prayers. He listens, and He communicates with us even when we do not understand His answer. Whether He says "yes" or "no," God always gives us the right answer because in His wisdom and love He knows what is best for us. Earthly parents do not always know the right answers to their childrens' requests, but God never makes mistakes. There are also times when a child's parents cannot give him the things he should have, but God can give His children anything that is good for them and He delights in doing it.

Sometimes God's answer may be neither "yes" nor "no," and it may come in the form of a new idea. I find that God often answers my prayers in a way that I never anticipated. I may think I know what is good for me, or for someone else, and I pray accordingly; but God, who knows the future as well as the present, sometimes guides me into another direction, one that turns out to be much better in the long run.

I have been particularly conscious about the wisdom of His direction in matters of giving money. As the trustee of a large foundation established by my father for religious benefactions, I have the responsibility of distributing a large sum of money each year. Naturally I get innumerable requests for donations, but many of them cannot be granted because they represent causes other than foreign mission work, the distribution of the Bible, orphanages and Bible institutes—causes to which the foundation's funds are limited. Even within the scope of the foundation, however, decisions must be made between different kinds of projects. This demands more than human judgment, and I always seek God's help in making these decisions.

Often I have had to decline a request for a project that appealed to me personally, because God made it clear to me that my judgment was faulty. There have been as many times when God convinced me that I should decide in favor of a project that did not appeal to me at first. Either way, God has always been right. He also appreciates the importance of time in making decisions and He always gives me an answer as soon as it is needed.

It is not surprising that when we accept the fact that God has such an intimate knowledge of our thoughts and lives, we may feel a little speechless when it comes to prayer. After all, how do we talk to God? What is there to say to an omniscient, omnipotent Spirit? Why would God be interested in hearing something He already knows? Here again, our communication with God is similar to the earthly child and his parent. When a child converses with his parent he does not do all the talking; he listens as well, for the parent has a lot of important things to say. Remember that prayer is a two-way communication, and we must spend more time listening to our spiritual Father than in telling Him about our needs in life. Surely we should not remain mute when we pray, for God likes to hear the sound of His children's voices even though they express themselves so poorly.

Sometimes, when we pray, we cannot put our thoughts into words, no matter how hard we try—and God understands. He has that marvelous capacity to feel the innermost thoughts of our hearts and He expresses them for us. Anyone who has ever felt this rare experience with his own child or with a friend can appreciate what a wonderful relationship it is.

In many of our prayers we tell God that we are praying in the name of Christ. In these words we claim the Sonship that is Christ's, for in our newly-born and newly-created spiritual nature we are one with Christ and therefore a child of God. Whether or not we say the words each time we pray, we must always remember our relationship to our Father if our prayers are to begin on the right foundation.

If we realize that we are children, as far as our spiritual nature is concerned, we will perhaps be able to realize why it is sometimes impossible for us to communicate with God. When a human child disobeys and does something he has been told not to do, communication between the child and his parent breaks down completely. The child must be disciplined, even when his disobedience comes from his desire for independence rather than his intention to do something wrong. For example, we would not say that a child is behaving in an evil way if he takes an extra piece of cake when he has already eaten enough, or when there may not be another piece for someone else, but his disobedience in itself is wrong and he must be brought to a realization of it. The parental discipline that follows a child's disobedience is not given to punish the child, but the disobedience itself cuts him off from the parental love he knew. Discipline, if properly applied, is corrective; it teaches the child that the parent must be obeyed and that the rebellious spirit within the child must be curbed. When the child can feel sorry for what he has done and can give up his disobedient behavior, he returns to the parent who receives him with love, thereby restoring their line of communication.

As human parents, we are often uncertain about disciplining our children. We are influenced by our own childhood, whether it seemed good or bad to us, and by our attempts to adjust to changing external conditions in life. I am sure from my own experience—and in some cases from my lack of applying discipline—that sensible discipline is a most important part of a child's development. True, we learn a lot from the suffering that comes from our own mistakes, and our children will have their own share of hard lessons, but that is no excuse for neglecting discipline. Our children will still make some mistakes, of course, but they will be able to learn something good from them. They will know when they have done something wrong, and their mistakes can make them return to the discipline they were taught. A child brought up without discipline flounders through life with no sense of direction.

Certainly parents must take the responsibility for disciplining children, but they will need the wisdom of God to apply it correctively. They can find this wisdom through prayer.

When we behave like wayward children, following our fleshly impulses into rebellion against God, we also break down our communication with Him and prayer becomes temporarily impossible. We are cut off from God's love and the discipline that follows disturbs our spiritual nature, putting it out of kilter—but it helps to bring us back to the right relationship.

Man must listen to God and not to other men, and many believers do not enjoy good spiritual health because they constantly follow human advice instead of God's instructions. God may be telling me to do or not to do certain things, while He may have an entirely different will for some of His other children. It is not for me to tell anyone else what he should do, nor should anyone else feel that God's direction in his life is also right for me. My instructions must come from God Himself, and it is my job to listen carefully to be sure I hear every word.

Our disobedience does not always come in the form of overt acts. Sometimes we rebel in our innermost thoughts and desires, but since God can see into our hearts He knows about them. While our secret desire may not be evil in itself, and may even be something we consider beneficial to mankind, if it becomes so important to us that it might interfere with our relationship with God, then it is a potential area of disobedience and God must reckon with it. Occasionally God tests our reactions to these desires, not because He needs to know what we will do, but because we must learn much more about ourselves.

We find it so hard to control our actions, and even harder to control our desires, some of which we do not even realize. How then are we to deal with this problem so that we do not constantly break off our communication with God? The Bible can give us the answer.

We human beings are so weak, so full of disobedience and rebellion, and we must confess our faults daily before we can come into the presence of God through prayer. In this way we can turn away from our disobedience toward God and His love.

A manufacturer knows that no operator, machine, or material is consistently perfect and he must always concern himself with the problem of controlling the high quality of his products. Our human problem is similar and we must constantly check on the materials and workmanship of our lives, making adjustments for our errors so that we can try to be perfect. If we are to be successful in catching our errors and correcting them, our quality-control system must be carried on daily, for our flesh never stops working against our spirit for an instant.

Just as the human parent is always ready to reestablish a loving relationship when the child returns to seek his love, God is always ready for us. How wonderful it is to return to such a loving Father who waits to dry our tears, to cleanse us of any filth we may have picked up, and to enfold us in His loving care!

If we have a daily need to confess our weaknesses, then we are not very strong creatures, certainly not strong enough to keep ourselves clean and right. Our weakness is something we should face, for when we do we fulfill another basic requirement for effective prayer.

We all have seen how infants learn to walk. They start across the room so confidently, then lose their balance, stumble, and fall down. As parents, we rush to pick up a fallen child and comfort him, encouraging him to try again. As spiritual infants, we have the child's problem. Thinking that we are stronger than we are, we try to do things on our own—and fall flat on our faces.

God does not handicap His children. He has given us abilities and He expects us to be able to do some things on our own; but many of life's situations demand more wisdom or strength than we will ever have, and we should be careful to distinguish between them. We have a Father who is ready to help us when our own abilities run short, if only we acknowledge our need for Him.

Being able to ask God's help and receiving it is not the full range of prayer, by any means. How often do we pray for something, find that our prayer is answered, and then feel horrified because we forgot to say "Thank You?" In our worldly lives, an expression of appreciation is so often omitted, and that is unfortunate. It gives such a wonderful quality of warmth to both the giver and receiver. We should never forget to say "Thank You" to God, for the Bible tells us that He expects our appreciation.

Thankfulness should be an essential element in our prayers. We can start to pray by giving thanks to God for what He has already done for us, and we can end by thanking Him for His attention and the answers He surely will give us.

We can be thankful for so many other things, too. Normally we think of expressing our appreciation for the nice things that happen to us—the pleasant experiences, the benefits that come to us—and no one is so poor that he cannot be grateful in this sense. What about the unpleasant parts of life—the misfortunes, the burdens, the worries, the suffering? Should we thank God for them, too? Shouldn't we learn to endure them without complaint and let it go at that? If we seek an answer from the Bible, we are told: ". . . in everything give thanks."

The meaning of these words, like the whole message of the Bible, is something that only a believer will understand. He knows that he is under the watchful care of the all-powerful, all-knowing, always-present God, and therefore he must conclude that there is a specific good purpose in everything that happens to him. He may never learn why he must bear his burden, but he trusts that it has something to do with the good of his spiritual nature. Perhaps God uses suffering to discipline the believer and bring him to his senses, to help his spirit grow, to teach him something that could not be taught in any other way.

In the construction of a good suit of clothes or a good pair of shoes, there are many operations the wearer cannot see and would not understand, but they made a considerable difference in durability and appearance over a long period of time. God, as the Maker of our spiritual entities, must do many things for us that are puzzling but necessary. Whatever his circumstances, the believer can truly be thankful for everything, and in his thankfulness he strengthens his relationship with God.

The Bible tells us to be instant in prayer and to pray without ceasing. This statement is somewhat curious, but in our day of "instant" everything we ought to understand what it means. Praying without ceasing means having an attitude of prayer, a constant readiness to communicate with God.

God is always with us and we must adapt our lives to His presence so that we are always ready to confer with Him about any matter that might come up. Whether we are alone or among other people, at home or away, at work or at leisure, sick or well, driving a car or riding in a plane, God is present. We cannot always carry on a conversation with Him, but if we let Him He can feed a constant stream of thoughts into our minds and hearts.

As we practice the art of prayer, we will gain an attitude of unceasing prayer. In all our feelings, problems, visions of opportunities, joys, and disappointments, we will have His presence and help. We will not shut Him out of our lives by disobeying or refusing to listen to Him.

We are the spiritual sons of Jesus Christ, members of an illustrious family, and everything we do should reflect credit on our spiritual Father, the Head of our family. Certainly when we pray we should ask for things that are worthy of God's attention. Our motivations are very important elements in the art of prayer and we would be very wrong to attempt to talk to God about matters that are selfish, unworthy, or just plain silly in His eyes.

Each person is motivated by different things and it is often hard for anyone to understand why he behaves as he does. We are very complex creatures and do not always recognize our reasons for wanting certain things. Our actions may be determined by our desire to gain materially, or to give others a better impression of ourselves, or to gratify unwholesome appetites. Our behavior may even be caused by our fears.

When we pray we must first ask ourselves why we are making our particular request. If we cannot give ourselves a straight answer, we will do better to keep the subject out of our prayers until our minds are clear about it. We should not be too hasty when we look at our reasons for petitioning God. I must admit that I have been pretty ashamed of myself at times when I woke up to the fact that I was about to ask God for something that turned out to be worthless when I examined it carefully.

Of course, we can never be sure we know our real reasons for doing anything. An unworthy desire may motivate some of our prayers, try as we may to avoid it, but God is never fooled. In His infinite wisdom He knows which of our requests are not in our best interests, and He will reject them.

The fundamental elements in the art of prayer cannot be fulfilled in the same way by all believers. Each of us is a unique individual, with a unique relationship to our Father, and each of us must establish our own lines of communication with Him. We can study the elements of prayer, but they alone will not teach us to pray. We will learn by experiencing these elements, gradually, through praying, and the process will be different for each one of us.

There are also many different prayer procedures and it is not necessary for all of us to follow the same pattern. People pray in various positions, at different times, in public, in private, and it is up to the individual to find the procedure that is best for him. Whatever pattern he prefers, the believer should be most concerned with acknowledging God as his spiritual Father and thanking Him for His goodness, and with confessing his human shortcomings and placing himself entirely within the will of God.

As children, most of us were taught to kneel when we prayed, and some people still prefer to pray in this position. It does not make a lot of difference, however, for the Bible describes prayers offered in all kinds of positions. We can stand, sit, kneel, or even lie down; our heads may be bowed or lifted up, our eyes open or closed, our prayers silent or voiced—God can hear our prayers from wherever we are, at any time of the day or night.

Some people find it helpful to set aside a regular time of the day for prayer, but that should not prevent us from praying throughout the day. All during our waking hours we can be breathing a silent prayer as we find the opportunity to do it. We must not take time only to talk to God; we must also turn to Him and listen to what He has to say to us.

I combine my praying with my Bible reading every night, just before I turn in, but some people may prefer to make their main prayer time in the morning or at some other time of day. As soon as I get up each morning, I start off the day with a short prayer, and join with my family for a devotional reading and prayer at breakfast. When I am eating in a restaurant or any other public place, I do not make a point of saying a prayer before my meal. I think the Bible teaches that prayer is a private matter, not a means of showing someone else how righteous we try to be.

There are times for public prayer, and a church service is certainly one of them. Many public meetings open with a dedicatory prayer, and if it is appropriate for the occasion I think it is fine. I have attended some meetings, however, where the prayer seemed to be part of the public show, and it was entirely out of place. Congress begins each day's session with a prayer, and they certainly need it. When a group sincerely asks God for guidance in the matters they are about to consider, they are acknowledging their human limitations, and such a prayer belongs on their agenda.

Many people wonder what they are supposed to do when a prayer is offered at a public meeting. Surely they should not merely listen when they have an opportunity to participate. If they make the spoken prayer their silent prayer, God will hear them as well as the speaker. If a listener feels that the person praying aloud is speaking only to impress the audience, he can make the time worthy of God's attention by praying silently about the matters in his own heart.

Public prayer is difficult because it is offered amid so many distractions, and it is often most effective when it is silent, with each person turning his own heart and mind to God. I have noticed that it takes almost a minute for an audience to forget about themselves and become aware of being in God's presence. When the period of silence has continued long enough to become almost oppressive, the prayer relationship becomes most effective for the individual.

Is it proper for us to pray for success in business? This is a personal matter for each of us to decide. It is certainly proper for us to ask for wisdom and strength to do what we ought to do, and to use our God-given abilities in the right way, and if this is truly our motive it has a place in our prayer life. We can and should pray about our family life, our social life, and any other area that uses our time and talents. Some people may think it strange that at the annual stockholders meeting of our corporation we start off with a prayer, but we feel that we want to thank God for all He has done for us and we know we need to seek His wisdom in conducting our affairs.

How heartwarming it is to be close enough to someone else to agree to pray for each other, or to join together in praying for someone or something else! There is a very special relationship between two people in a prayer partnership, and the Bible tells us that God promises particular attention to prayers made by two or more people who ask His help on a matter.

I have found that a written prayer list is very helpful. I use it to remind myself to be thankful for everything, and to review my day and check up on my shortcomings. I also keep a list of people I want to remember in my prayers. I am surprised that I constantly need to be reminded to be thankful for everything, even for the unpleasant, disappointing parts of my life. I am not so surprised that I need to keep track of my faults every day—my acts of self-pride, or feelings of self-righteousness, or my unkindnesses, evil thoughts, hostilities, and intemperances. I feel as if I have taken a cleansing bath when I admit them to God in my prayers and realize anew that I am still His beloved child, in spite of my lack of merit.

Prayer is a form of labor for our spiritual Father, and not too many believers realize that they are under an obligation to pray for many things. We have such vast power available to us, but we do not make the best use of it. Because we do not know how to pray very well, and because we spend so much time praying for ourselves and our families, our prayers are not nearly as effective as they should be.

It is true that God has given each of His spiritual children certain gifts, and we are quite different from each other, but we do share one ability in common. Each of us has the ability to be useful in prayer, to serve as a channel for God's power to come into this world. In this way God's Word, the spiritual seed, can propagate itself and come to life in new spiritual creations. Not all of us can be active in church work, or contribute money, or preach, or heal, but we can all pray.

Praying is not easy. It requires practice, time, and an outpouring of the inner things in one's life. When the heart is truly burdened with the need, prayer is labor in the real sense of the word; but it is a glorious labor, a gratifying, uplifting experience, and a wonderful source of joy.

13

Follow God Through the Bible

Anyone who attempts to study the amazing library of books in the Bible is setting himself a hard task. No matter how well his intellectual abilities have served him in other areas of his life, they will be of little help here. The Bible speaks to the needs of the soul, and a man cannot understand it unless he has the spiritual keys to its message.

If we can accept the Bible as the truth, then we are in possession of the first key, but our acceptance must go beyond our conviction that everything we read in the Bible is God's Word and therefore valid. We must accept to the point of obedience. If God speaks to us through His Word and tells us to do something, then we must be prepared to do it even though it may seem hard or unimportant. Our readiness to follow God's will, as it is made clear to us, also enables God to guide us to an ever-deeper understanding of the Bible. On the other hand, if God knows that we are not going to follow His instructions, then it is hardly likely that He will try to clarify them.

I know what it is to experience God's will in my life. I also know that my rebellious human nature has sometimes doubted the wisdom of that will. I remember a time, early in my business career, when our company was presented with the opportunity to acquire a large company on quite favorable terms. The offer seemed to hold a lot of advantages—not only to us, but to several other companies—and the decision rested in the hands of one person, a very toughminded individual who was much older than I. I was so anxious to say and do the right things that I think I stretched my prayer principles a little when I sought God's guidance in those days.

I never learned exactly why the decision went against our company. Money was not the important factor, but the man who made the decision apparently thought better of someone in another company than he did of me. I was very disappointed, but after a few mental gulps I told myself that I had done the best I could. The opportunity was simply not for me, and I wasn't going to worry about it.

Not quite two years later, some serious problems came to light in the firm we had sought to acquire, and it turned out to be most fortunate that we did not succeed. Was it a coincidence? I don't think so. I believe that God protected me from my own desires and faulty wisdom, and I have always been grateful for it.

We hold a second key to understanding the Bible if we are able to communicate with God through prayer. Our abilities and education can teach us so many things about business, medicine, literature, mathematics, music, art, science, and all other human affairs, but we need to seek God's powers in our study of the Bible. Only His Spirit can teach us about spiritual matters which, while they do not contradict human matters, are in an entirely different realm and require a different approach.

If we pray for understanding, and if a good part of our prayer is spent in listening, God will explain His Word to us and help to find the truths that we alone could never find. This is another good reason why we must learn how to pray, practice the art of it, and become proficient in communicating with our Heavenly Father.

Time is the third spiritual key and perhaps the most difficult one to obtain. Time is the stuff of which life is made, and we should not waste it if we are to enjoy life. We must spend time reading the Bible, we must spend time praying about it, and we must spend time doing what the Lord tells us to do, if we are to understand the Scriptures. If we give enough of our time to these things, we can be in tune with God's spiritual leading, and He can then speak to our hearts in many ways. If we are in the jet stream of the Spirit, we will receive the power that comes from it.

We can also use our time well by listening to the ministers and teachers in our churches, and by reading literature that relates to Biblical study. Of course, this takes up some of those precious hours each of us spends on the earth, but if we want to understand the Bible we must take advantage of every opportunity God offers us.

Unfortunately, some of our churches do not give us much that is worthwhile in relation to the Bible. Some are so involved with social problems, reforming the world, obtaining publicity, and organizing projects, that the Bible is far down on their priority list.

Each year in our business we revise and extend our five-year, long-range plan, reconfirming and refining our objectives. We do this because we have found that we will not get effective results from our efforts if some of us are pulling in one direction and some of us in another. We have a better chance to carry out our plans if we constantly keep our objectives before us.

Confusion about an objective is in my opinion one of the great problems in our churches today. What is the purpose of the church as an organization? Many people feel that the church should use its influence to reform the world, to promote the general welfare, or to exert pressure on political governments. Many others, equally conscientious, hold opposite views. Both are human definitions, and the real answer to the question can only be found by going back to the Bible and finding out what it has to say about the early church congregation during the time of the apostles.

The Bible tells us that the original churches were very active. They sought to reach individuals and plant the seed of the Word of Christ in them so that new Christian spiritual beings might be born. They nourished these people, spiritually and physically, helping them to grow in grace and the knowledge of the Lord. The funds they collected supported their ministers, the missionaries they sent out, and the poor among the church members. As a congregation, they provided a group with whom others could join in prayer and worship.

Also interesting are some of the things those churches did not do. They did not attempt to use their corporate influence to change laws or reform the government—even though they were persecuted by many governments—and there is no record that they either sought or gained political favor. They did not mount crusades to reform the general citizenry. In their day there was much wickedness in the world, as there is now, but they were concerned about the discipline of their own members, not about a universal welfare program. They did not consider themselves so wise as to be able to revise the gospel message according to their own human philosophy. They did not have *any* church buildings, but met in small groups, in homes, in the open fields, or even in caves. Their organizational structure was very limited and there were no recreational or social programs.

The proper objectives of the church are set forth in the Bible, but we lose sight of them when we cover them over with our own interpretations. If the church will accept God's definition of its job—and if it will stick to that job—it will become far stronger and more effective in reaching the will of God.

I do not mean that we are wasting our time in a church that does not adhere strictly to its proper purpose. This problem exists in many other areas of life and it is almost impossible to avoid it. When we go to school, we spend many hours on useless material, some of it having little or nothing to do with education, and perhaps only a few of our teachers can really impart knowledge. Some people may have the same complaint about their church, but they should not give up the time they spend there. Just as the disciplines we develop in school often turn out to be more useful than we realized, so we often find that time spent listening to religious leaders and speakers can be useful in ways we did not expect.

Many times, while listening to a minister, I have found myself thinking about an entirely different subject. Perhaps a word he used, or a phrase, or an illustration triggered a thought that somehow gave me a new insight into a question that had been bothering me. The same thing has been true in my reading, when an unrelated idea is occasionally developed because my mental processes are stirred up or made more receptive by what I have read.

Time is a difficult key to obtain because so many of us are afraid to lose time. We think we have so little, but by using it more efficiently we can, in a sense, stretch it out. I find that the time I spend in studying the Bible, praying, attending church services, and reading does not really keep me from other desirable activities. In other words, I believe that the Spirit of God in some mysterious way takes care of my time problems so that the hours spent on religious activities do not reduce my time for other kinds of living. In fact, the reverse seems to be true in my case, and I have had more time than most people I know to live a full life.

I have spent more than an average amount of time on

my business work, because I enjoy it, and I estimate that I have averaged at least sixty hours a week at my job—and a fourteen-hour day is not an unusual event with me. I like to travel, too, and have been around the world twice, traveled extensively in Europe, the Middle East, the Far East, Australia, Africa, Latin America, and North America. Reading is an important part of my life, and I have found the time to read widely in many fields of literature. I have enjoyed my family, and have a wide circle of friends and acquaintances. Although it is a real chore for me, I have made a good many speeches, when necessary, and have spent time in politics and community affairs. I even watch a lot of sporting events. I enjoy music, but it wasn't until I was over forty years old that I took the time to learn how to play the piano—after a fashion. Several years ago I discovered the pleasure of visiting art galleries and I have become an amateur collector of abstract paintings. All these activities give me enjoyment and make my time valuable, but I do not believe I would have time to do more if I eliminated all the time I spend on my religious life.

When a person has the three spiritual keys, he can put them to better use by organizing his study of the Bible. Originally the Book was written in ancient languages, by many different men, but its real Author is God and its truth is for all men and all ages. Although produced over many hundreds of years, it is a unified whole and the Old Testament is just as vital to our understanding as the New Testament. Through the centuries, the original manuscript was separated into chapters and verses, for convenience in reference, and translated into many modern languages. Most of us read the Bible in translation and it is interesting to compare different versions. Sometimes a comparison may open up a new approach for study.

Some people study the Bible by starting at the beginning, analyzing it verse by verse, and going straight through to the end. Others refer to study specific subjects and, with the aid of a reference book, look up all the related passages. There are several other study methods and it is worthwhile to try them. Even when a person finds one method that seems to suit him, it is good to vary the approach occasionally.

In my own study, I read the Bible through completely each year, starting at the beginning and going straight through. In the past I have sometimes followed schedules that took me through the Book twice during the year, or once through the Old Testament and twice through the New Testament. For the past several years I have read three chapters every weekday and five chapters on Sunday, a schedule which provides for one complete reading each year.

If you have ever taken the time to reread a favorite book, you have probably known the pleasure of discovering things you overlooked the first time. The Bible, however, offers new revelations to the serious student no matter how many times it is read. Its truth is so profound that I have never found it to be repetitious, and in fact I approach each new reading with eagerness.

When questions arise in my reading—and they often

do—I search for the answers in other parts of the Bible and in other books, and I listen to many speakers. I have often found help from these sources, but my greatest source of information has been God Himself. Through prayer I have been able to bring my questions to God and His answers have been my best guide to understanding the Bible. When He does not give me an answer, I know that He has His reasons.

14

God's Methods
in Past Ages

*My business experience has taught me that a com-*pany can be managed properly only if it is divided and subdivided so that the chief executive can communicate with each of its parts and guide their activities. In other words, it must be organized. When it comes to studying the Bible—or any other body of knowledge—we must subdivide it into its parts, analyze their meanings, and learn how they fit together.

There are many ways to organize a study of the Bible, with many pros and cons about each of them. One of the best Bible students I have known says that he gains a deeper understanding of all the Scriptures through studying them in the light of the second coming of Christ, and it is true that many questions throughout the Bible can be answered by relating them to the second coming. Some people may concentrate on the Biblical prophecies, and while we are not yet able to comprehend their full meanings, they are a fascinating subject. By knowing more about them we can understand more about some of the events happening in the world today.

Each person should try various approaches to find the one that is best for him. I can describe only my experience with God's Word, and I expect that every other child of God will have a different, unique story to tell.

I have been using the dispensational approach to the Bible because it has been the most helpful one for me, although some people have been critical of it. A dispensation refers to an age, or a period in history, when God made certain revelations to man in a way that was particularly suited to that period of time. Some of these dispensations ended abruptly; some of them began before a previous one ended; not all of them have yet ended.

I believe the entire Bible to be the revealed truth of God, but the dispensational approach explains why some of God's instructions applied specifically to one age and not to another. For study purposes we can divide the Bible into seven dispensations, or seven different ages in which God dealt differently with mankind; and if we can learn why God made each of these revelations at certain stages in man's development, then perhaps we can learn something about His dealings with us today.

Some people may not want to spend their time studying an age that seems to have no relationship to the present one, but we cannot learn the whole truth about God, man, or the Bible by skipping occasional chapters. We are no different from the first man, no matter how far we may think we have come. As we study each dispensation, we will see how many other ages of men also thought they were different until they responded to God in the same old rebellious way. If we consider only the forms of rebellion, it is true that some of them might be considered a little out of date. If we look deeper and discover the evil motive behind them, we will find that it is always the same.

In the first dispensation God created man as an innocent creature, without a knowledge of good or evil. He was placed in an ideal environment, offered the opportunity to become immortal, given the freedom to choose to obey or disobey his Creator, and warned of the penalty for disobedience. When man chose to disobey, he fell under the curse of God, lost the chance to become immortal, was evicted from his ideal environment, and condemned to sorrow, toil, and physical death.

We do not know how long this dispensation lasted, and time may have been accounted differently in those days, but we can see its application in our lives today. We have inherited the first man's rebelliousness as well as his penalty for it. As Adam was composed of dust and sentenced to return to dust, so will we.

Cast out of his environment, man entered another age, a second dispensation. He now had a knowledge of good and evil, and by that knowledge came conscience. No longer an innocent creature, man became responsible for doing what was right and not doing what was wrong. His thoughts as well as his actions were to be guided by his conscience which had been born of his experience of defying the will of God.

Apparently, man was still permitted to approach

God, but under new and special conditions. He had to make an acceptable offering, a sacrifice, to symbolize his allegiance and submission to God. The Bible also tells us that God was never fooled, for He accepted the sacrifice only when He was pleased with the inner spirit of the man who offered it.

Man failed as miserably in the second dispensation as he did in the first. Even though he knew the difference between right and wrong, he refused to accept the responsibility for his behavior and deliberately did what was wrong. Letting his imagination run wild, man seemed to go out of his way to indulge in evil.

The second dispensation should not seem alien to us, for we go through a similar stage in our own development. We can all appreciate man's struggle with his conscience because it still goes on today. Even those of us who listen to our consciences are well aware that our imaginations are vile and evil, while our actions may variously appear to be proper. Perhaps those who are able to stifle the voice of their conscience, or close their ears to it, are in worse trouble.

When God saw the results of man's continuing disobedience, He decided to destroy him. He planned to begin a new dispensation and He picked out one family with whom He could make a new start.

Mankind, with the exception of that one family, was destroyed by a flood such as the world has not seen before or since. The deluge was not a natural but a supernatural event, and God had prepared Noah and his menagerie to survive it. My personal belief is that the environmental weather of the world then was entirely different than it is now, with great masses of clouds continually surrounding the earth. By turning loose all the vapor in the clouds and opening up subterranean fountains, God allowed an unprecedented amount of water to envelop the earth, completely destroying its surface and those who lived on it.

I am well aware that many so-called enlightened people cannot accept the fact of the flood or the miraculous survival of the group who huddled in the ship that took Noah one hundred years to build. They really accept all kinds of scientific marvels they cannot understand, but they draw the line when it comes to supernatural things. How ironic that antideluvian men could not possibly have believed in television, but they could believe in some other things that many people cannot accept today!

No one believes only those things his mind can take apart and put together again. Having experienced the truth of the Bible time and time again, I am perfectly willing to accept the supernatural events in it, just as I am willing to accept some of the "modern miracles" of science, even when I can't possibly understand them. I do not believe that this makes me an irrational person; it simply acknowledges that some things are beyond my limited ability to analyze.

The third dispensation began with a special revelation of God to one family of people in a clean new world. It was an age characterized by the institution of human government. For the first time God gave authority to certain men and allowed them to rule over other men, to direct them as to what they could and could not do. Those men were selected by God and given the knowledge to govern.

We can see that this dispensation overlaps subsequent dispensations and is still in effect today. That is why Paul tells us that our present human governments are ordained of God and must therefore be obeyed by men. We may wonder why these governments are permitted to continue in power in spite of their abundant corruption, weakness, stupidity, and falseness, and why we should obey them, but there are implicit limitations in that command. For instance, if a government should tell us to disobey God, we must refuse.

God, who has all power, has delegated to human government the power to take human life for judicial reasons. This is the supreme function of government. From this power to take life come all the other powers of government over the people governed, and it is therefore inaccurate to base arguments against capital punishment upon an interpretation of the Bible. The very existence of human governments is proof of their authority to take the life of a man whose disobedience has invoked that penalty. Whether or not a government uses this power is an entirely different matter.

Although God gave men the authority to govern the world, it is evident that they have misused it badly. They have governed not for God but for their own selfish purposes. Once again, men failed to accept their responsibility, refusing to listen to God, and they will continue to suffer the tragedy of bad government until God puts an end to the third dispensation.

The world has seen various forms of government, and

men are always sure that their problems will be solved if only an honest man can be found, or if only the right system of checks and balances is used, or if only all the wealth can be turned over to the government. A study of world history, however, reveals that the usual form of government, in country after country, is vacillating, corrupt, extravagant, and incompetent. As a matter of fact, when we become disheartened over our own governmental problems, we can find some comfort in going back over the history of other governments.

A fourth dispensation began to emerge while the dispensation of government was still in effect. From the descendants of Noah God selected another special person, Abraham, and to him He made a further revelation and some amazing promises.

Abraham lived among people who worshiped idols, but somehow God spoke to him and Abraham listened. Abraham was a man of faith, but not by accident; since every good thing men have comes from God, Abraham's faith was also God-given. It was a new spiritual creation planted in his human body by God Himself. Of course, Abraham did not understand why God had selected him, but that was not important to a man who trusted God and was willing to obey Him. As he obeyed, Abraham found out that he was beginning to understand many things.

God told Abraham to leave his city, his family, his friends, and go to a place he had never seen. God would show him the way and there He would make of him a great nation. Abraham went, not knowing where God was leading him, yet his faith was strong enough to face all the possible dangers he might encounter along the way.

God made more than one promise to Abraham. He was to become not only a great name and nation, but through him a blessing would come to all families of the earth. Abraham accepted these promises on faith, for he did not live to see their fulfillment. The dispensation of promise lasted as long as the heirs of Abraham remained in the land where God had led their father. When they left and went into Egypt, the age ended but the promises were not withdrawn. They were to be completed at a later time, and we who are living today, nearly four thousand years later, have a better understanding of what they meant. We acknowledge the name of Abraham and can attest that a great nation came forth from him. We have the fulfillment of the third promise in Christ, a descendant of Abraham according to the flesh, through whom blessing will come to all families of the earth.

15

Prophecy Unfolds
in Israel

Abraham had a grandson named Jacob and the story of his descendants is one of the most amazing episodes in history. Jacob was renamed Israel ("Prince of Peace") by God, and from his twelve sons came the tribes of the Israelites. The Jews descended from three of the twelve sons (Judah, Benjamin, and Levi); they have continued to this day as a separate people with a remarkable history of achievement, cultural development, and cruel persecution, while the other descendants of Jacob have lost their identity among other peoples. But God still knows them and where they are. The Bible teaches that they will be identified at the proper time, and when that happens it is quite possible that you and I will be among them.

We are all familiar with the story of Joseph, one of Jacob's sons, who became a prime minister of Egypt after an extraordinary series of adventures that took him from the land of his fathers. He was able to give food to his people during a time of great famine, but when they saw the plentiful land of Egypt they decided to settle there, leaving the land God had given to Jacob and ending the dispensation of promise. For a while they prospered in Egypt, multiplying in number, until the Egyptians, fearing their growing power, gradually enslaved them.

The Israelites suffered under the hardships of slavery until they were led by Moses to rebel against their masters. In a vast body they moved once more toward the land God had promised to Abraham and his children, and again they were incapable of carrying out God's commands. Complaining, willful, ungrateful, and disobedient, they were sentenced to wander for forty years in the desolate land between Egypt and Palestine. Many of them died; those who survived the rugged existence were hardened, determined people, ready to reach and conquer Palestine, the land of promise.

In His wonderful provision, God used the wilderness years to prepare the Israelites for their future national home. He began by giving them a body of regulations known as the Law, a detailed set of procedures which would set them apart from all other nations of the world. This Law marked the beginning of a new dispensation in which God set aside a special family of people to receive a new revelation. Abandoning the rest of the world's human beings to their own evil desires, God chose the descendants of one man to be His people.

God gave the Law to the Israelites in three parts, each of them carefully detailed. Besides the commandments with which we are so familiar, there were judgments to govern the people's social life, and ordinances concerning their religious life. In the most explicit terms God promised that if the people would obey His voice by keeping the Law, they would become a holy nation, a peculiar treasure to Him. The terrible penalties for disobedience were made equally clear.

The Israelites made a commitment to God when they agreed to live according to the Law, and they did it voluntarily, but they continued to follow the desires of the flesh. In spite of special revelations from God and the repeated warnings of the prophets, they rushed headlong into disobedience, breaking all commandments, judgments, ordinances. There was always a small group who remained true to God, but they were not enough to overcome the sordidness and disgrace that colored the story of the Israelites.

The Bible tells us the whole story, both the good and the bad parts. If it had been humanly written and conceived, we would probably know only the nice side of the record, for it is a human tendency to gloss over the ugly side of life. Instead, God has given us a realistic Book that speaks in strong language.

The story of David and Bathsheba and the murder of Uriah is an example of plain truth in plain language, with no attempt made to cover up the terrible sin of a great king of Israel in its early history as a free nation. Devastating as it was in his own life, David's sin is even more shocking because it was symptomatic of people who seemed to wallow in evil at the same time that they scrupulously observed the ritualistic forms of religion.

Once again God's judgment fell upon His wayward

children and they were taken captive by the Chaldeans, a Gentile nation. The captivity ushered in the "times of the Gentiles," which continues until this day and will not end until Jesus Christ returns to earth a second time as a powerful Leader. A second part of the judgment scattered the Israelites to all parts of the world to meet with persecution in the very nations where they sought refuge. At a later time, the Bible tells us, they would be forced by the severity of the persecution to return to their national home.

The fifth dispensation did not end with the captivity and dispersion of the Israelites but continued until the first coming of Christ. Perfect in every way, obedient to all God's commands, He fulfilled the Law that rebellious man had defied.

There is a strange feeling among the Jews today in regard to the land of Palestine, and many of them are drawn to it for reasons they do not understand. After the Second World War they were offered havens other than Palestine—some of them much more desirable— but they would have only the land which their fathers had left so long ago.

For centuries before the First World War, Palestine had been controlled by Turkey. After Turkey was defeated in the war, Palestine became a League of Nations mandate under assignment to Great Britain and was intended to provide a refuge for Jews who were being forced to leave their homes in other countries. The Turks are Moslems, but not Arabs, and Palestine had long since passed from domination by any Arab nation even before it had been controlled by Turkey.

Many Arabs lived in Palestine, however, and they, as well as the Arab nations bordering the country, resented the prospect of any increase in the Jewish population. There was constant turmoil between the two groups, and when I first visited Palestine in 1939 the British were finding it hard to keep order. They were caught between the Arab nations who were pressuring them to keep the Jews out of Palestine, and the Zionists who wanted them to live up to the commitments made under the League of Nations mandate.

After World War II, homeless Jews from all over the world surged toward Palestine and the conflict between the Jews and Arabs came to a head in a war. The result was a division of the country into the Jewish area —Israel—and the Arab area—Trans Jordan—the split going right through the city of Jerusalem. And so it remains today.

The Arab refugees who left Israel gathered in the desert near the Dead Sea where they have been supported by donations from many countries, including the United States. Their unsettled existence, where they eat without working, has become a way of life for them, and in my observation their economic conditions seem to be far better than a good percentage of the Arab populations of Egypt, Trans Jordan, Syria, or Iraq, where a strong adherence to traditional ways offers little material or educational advantages. In these Arab countries the past has such a strong grip on the present that women still do most of the labor because it is considered beneath the dignity of men.

The contrast between the Jews of Israel and their

Arab neighbors is striking. I have been to Israel several times and have been impressed by the enormous energy and determination of the Jews as they moved into a barren land and transformed it inch by inch into a productive, truly civilized society. Their dedication to their vision of the future can be measured by their willingness to commit minds, hearts, tools, and even bare hands to it. Realizing that not all their problems can be solved through material achievements, they are stressing the importance of education in their future.

After the division of Palestine, Jewish people from all parts of the world poured into Israel. Feeding all these new people, providing them with work and the means to support themselves, were only some of the problems that threatened the nation's survival, but the Israelis stuck to their policy that no Jew would be turned away from the country. With hostile countries on all sides of them, the people also had to prepare themselves to resist possible attacks. An industrial development program was one of their most urgent needs, and that was how our company—and many others—came into the picture.

Through many business contacts I have had a chance to get to know the Jewish people quite well. Several years ago, some Israeli businessmen asked our company to help them set up a shoe manufacturing plant in their country and to train workers in operating it. We agreed, and for almost two years our representatives lived and worked in Israel, teaching people to operate machines that were completely strange to them and trying to overcome a particularly difficult language problem. The workers in that one plant had come from as many as eighteen different countries and communication was almost impossible at first, especially in technical matters. When our representatives realized that they could instruct by demonstration rather than by words alone, they found the answer to the problem. The Israelis have a wonderful spirit of enthusiasm and a great desire to learn, and they made rapid progress.

The Biblical prophecies regarding the Israelites are so extraordinary in themselves that they are convincing proof of the truth of the Bible. Many of the Jews who have returned to Israel are almost, if not in fact, atheists, without any realization that everything they are doing now was written in detail thousands of years ago. It is stated in the Bible that these people would be drawn back to the land in unbelief, and this is what is happening. True, many orthodox Jews in Israel believe in God and in the promises made to the children of Israel during the days of Moses, but I believe that they are definitely in the minority. Although they do not accept the divinity of Jesus Christ, the Bible prophesies that their eyes will be opened on this subject some day in the future.

The events in Israel since the end of World War II are fascinating when viewed against the background of the Old Testament words that describe them. They offer an amazing perspective for anyone who reads them with an open mind. Through eyes widened by the power of God, we can see the present evidence of a judgment that came upon a people centuries ago when they abused the Law they had received from God Himself.

16

God's Methods
in This Age

*Man, on the basis of his human merits, deserves noth-*ing from God but the death his disobedience has earned him. Instead he receives the opportunity to live eternally. How often men have thought they have done something to merit God's mercy, yet these very thoughts reveal how little they know about God's immeasurable love!

We are living now in the sixth dispensation, a time when God's grace is at work among men. It began with the death and resurrection of Jesus Christ, God's most profound demonstration of His love and mercy toward men, and it provides a way for men to be born anew into a spiritual existence. The new spiritual body—like the body of Christ when He arose from the grave—comes to life in those who accept and receive His Word. It has nothing to do with the individual's merits, or with the good things he does or doesn't do, but it has everything to do with God's grace.

The dispensation of grace is a time when God's mercy and kindness are preparing men's hearts to receive His Word which will then grow into the new spiritual existence. It depends entirely upon man's willingness to accept such a gift of love.

Any good deeds done by a believer are the results of the new spiritual life within him—that is, any good deeds of value. Does this mean that a nonbeliever is incapable of doing something good? Most of us would object to such a statement, but I believe that if we examine the good deeds of nonbelievers we will find they have not had any lasting effects in the world and are often canceled out by other deeds motivated by purely human desires. As a matter of fact, some people think that so-called do-gooders are responsible for much of the trouble in the world, in spite of their seemingly good intentions and sincerity. Of course, there are a lot of believers among the "do-gooders," and it might come as a surprise to find that they don't get any better results, but they are people whose spiritual embryos are very young and still under the domination of the fleshly tendencies. In our painful struggle with our conscience it often happens that we mistake evil desires for something good.

One of the greatest misconceptions about the spiritual rebirth is that it causes the believer to live a sinless life. This is so far from the truth that it is a serious obstacle to understanding the conflict that goes on between the growing embryo and the human nature that makes every brutal effort to crush it. As the spiritual being matures within a man, it gives him more and more strength to fight against his flesh, but as long as the physical body exists it continues to wage the war.

Every believer knows that he is neglecting some things he ought to do and giving in to some temptations he ought to resist.

Possibly a similar misunderstanding accounts for the sharp criticism aimed at the church by many nonbelievers. I have heard some say that churches are attended by a lot of hypocrites, sadfaced pessimists, puritanical busybodies, and impostors—which implies that only "good" people should attend church. The truth is quite another story. When I go to church, I do not go because I am better than anyone else, as far as human life is concerned. I go because I need help, because I am not perfect, and because my spiritual nature needs the nourishment I can find there. If I fit any of the labels that are pinned on church members, then I need even more help.

I'll admit that the churches are open to a lot of criticism—and I could mention a few points that nonbelievers have missed—but I know of many more unpleasant faults among groups outside the church. I have been associated with several business, political, social, and community organizations, and I have always run into some characters whom I disliked, or even detested, but not to the point where I lost sight of the worthwhile efforts of the group as a whole.

Many believers are aware of the problems that exist in the churches today but they recognize them as some of the events that the Bible predicts for the dispensation of grace. This age, we are told, will culminate in a time when the powers of evil will seem to predominate in the world, and there will be tribulation such as men have never seen. Human beings will observe a form of godliness but will deny its power and will indulge in every conceivable evil. They will ever be learning yet never coming to a knowledge of the truth. The church itself, while claiming to serve God, will turn away from Him, concealing its surrender to the powers of evil beneath the guise of reforms and good works.

The end days will be perilous ones, and I believe that we are in the midst of them now. The indications are obvious. We can see them in some of our theologians who seem to follow a form of godliness but deny its power. In their never-ending, never-finding search for truth, and while they probe, define, and argue, they have lost the power to plant the Word of God as seed in the hearts of human beings. Feeling that they must conform to the scientific outlook—which cannot accept what is not apparent to all—they have denied God's miraculous power, discarded many portions of His Word, and come to the conclusion that God is a myth.

The people—theologians or others—who try to look at life from a scientific viewpoint are even more foolish than those they imitate. They would be quite startled to read the papers published by the American Scientific Affiliation, an organization of outstanding scientists who are also true believers in God and the Bible, and who have experienced the new spiritual birth. These men realize that science is not the answer to everything and that there are more things beyond its scope than within it.

Today there are false teachers among us, just as the

Bible predicted, and they are hard to detect because they masquerade as angels of light. We can recognize them by their refusal to accept the divinity of Jesus Christ, but even in this they are sometimes very subtle. Some of them will say that Jesus was divine, yet if pressed further they will contend that all men are divine because they were created by God in His image. In other words, in their hair-splitting fashion they are saying that Jesus was a great Man—but just another human being. Others will say that the whole matter of Christ's divinity is not important—what really counts is His life, His philosophy. Don't believe these people, no matter how plausibly they may phrase their words or how great is their reputation or influence. They are false teachers, and you don't have to take my word for it. Take the Bible's word, God's Word. Read a little further and discover what will happen to false teachers at the end of this dispensation, and you will no longer wonder why they do not believe in the dispensations! The test for a true teacher is his acceptance of the fact that Jesus Christ was miraculously divine, was born of a virgin, lived a sinless life, was slain by crucifixion, and arose alive from the dead.

The Bible is quite specific about a lot of other events during the last days of this dispensation, but it gives us no information as to when the end will come. We are advised to be on the lookout for it at all times, and from the way the world appears today, we had better watch carefully. Some of the descriptions of the probable effects of atomic warfare in so much of modern literature bear a deadly comparison with the "perilous times" mentioned in the Bible, and certainly this is a means of devastation that could not have been foreseen two thousand years by the human writers of the Scriptures. Only a Divine Power possessed of all knowledge could have foreseen the details of such a holocaust, just as He foresaw the other features of our contemporary world.

The human race will not completely destroy itself, but men do hold the power to bring upon themselves a time of suffering that is beyond their present ability to imagine. If they should continue to fail in their responsibilities—as they have done since the time of Adam—they will witness the fulfillment of a prophecy they have refused to heed.

God assures us that the believers remaining on the earth at the end of the dispensation of grace will be taken out of the world before the time of tribulation. We are not told exactly how this will be done, but since it will be a miraculous event we probably would not understand it even if we knew the details. How they will go, and where, are not important to believers—it is enough that they have God's promise.

17

The Age Ahead of Us

When Jesus Christ was taken up into heaven after His resurrection, the people who were watching were told by two messengers from God that He would return to the world in exactly the same way that He was taken up. Is it so hard to understand why the disciples thought the event would happen in their lifetime? Since then, faithful believers in every generation have been awaiting the glorious return of the Son of God in His power.

He will not come again as He came the first time. He has walked among us as a Man, with humility and with persuasion, but He will return as our King, with supernatural forces at His command.

In a way, we might think of the present world as a province in rebellion against the Ruler of the infinite universe, and the Kingdom age as a restoration of His divine power on earth.

Following the terrible destruction that will end the dispensation of grace, Christ will descend from heaven to usher in the dispensation of the fullness of time—the Kingdom age—amid the wreckage of the earth. It is very likely that the world power systems will have destroyed each other by that time, but if they exist in any form they will then be swept away with the chaos of their deeds. A new world government will then be formed, ruled by a divine King, and He will conduct the affairs of the world with perfect skill and wisdom, bringing it into a period of peace and prosperity such as it has never known.

Can we possible imagine how life will be in the Kingdom age? I don't think so, for we won't find any similarities in our life today. Can we conceive of a world without suffering, injustice, crime, sickness, poverty, heartache, loneliness, fear, insecurity, weakness, jealousy, pride, covetousness? That is how men will live under the leadership of God Himself in the person of Jesus Christ. Even the animals will know a different way of life, for they will no longer fight with each other or with men. We are not told what carnivorous animals will eat, but this is only one of thousands of little questions that come to mind when one contemplates the future age. We do not need the answers now. God knows them, and He will reveal them to us at the proper time.

The Bible states clearly that death will not be destroyed until after the Kingdom age, but during Christ's reign men will regain the longevity that existed during the first generations of mankind. According to Isaiah, a man of one hundred years will be considered an infant. Death will not be destroyed during the Kingdom age—this the Bible explains clearly—yet we are left to wonder what form it will take, since so many of its agents will be eliminated. Not until the Kingdom age ends, after one thousand years, and the fullness of time begins, will death be destroyed. Then we will enter a new kind of existence as spiritual beings.

To the watchful eye, the signs on the horizon of world events indicate that we are in the time of trouble that is to occur before the return of Christ. Beyond the return of the Israelites to Palestine, and the possibility of atomic warfare, some recent scientific developments are fitting like pieces of a puzzle into the Biblical prophecies. For example, Scripture tells us that when Jesus returns in glory, every eye will be able to see Him. Until the past few years, that seemed impossible, considering the spherical shape of the earth, but now we have communication satellites in fixed positions so that we can see what is happening in all parts of the world. We can hardly presume that the second coming will be televised, for Christ does not need man's little gadgets to make His presence known. We can, however, be humbled by the realization that some of the things we take for granted today would have been considered miracles a few years ago. In our prideful human way, we think we know all the answers, and we fail to see that our "discoveries" have existed since the beginning of time. We stumble over things; we do not create them. If Christ delays His coming we will gradually stumble over a few more things, but they will still be like drops in the bucket compared to the knowledge of God.

I suppose that some people might say to themselves, after reading this book, "How can a sensible, down-to-earth businessman believe such far-out, mystical, improbable things?" I am willing to take the quizzical glance, to be regarded as a fanatic, a crackpot, an unrealistic kind of person. It is part of the struggle that goes on inside any believer. We are under great pressure from society to conform to the accepted beliefs and practices of the majority, and our human nature wants to gain the good opinion of other people, but a believer cannot keep his faith a secret. Sometimes, when I express my beliefs to others, I embarrass them. While they will concede that every man has a perfect right to his own ideas, they shake their heads, thinking, "This sort of thing just isn't done by anyone in the know." Apparently it is all right to have your own views as long as you don't talk about them. Above all, don't flaunt them in the faces of those who may misunderstand or ridicule you!

I have known many successful people in the fields of business, finance, education, religion, politics, and I have found myself in the midst of a variety of groups. I think I am quite well aware of their mores and practices, but I can't submerge my own views when they differ from those around me. Sometimes my independence is taken for foolishness and my nonconformity is pitied. As far as I am concerned, I was brought up to develop strong convictions of my own, and I must do such things that seem right to me, even when they do not coincide with the best wishes of my friends. I believe in the truth of the Bible, and I agree with the words of Henry Goodpasture, an attorney and a Bible teacher in my hometown, that it should be "boldly asserted and stoutly maintained."

I have no desire to impose my views on anyone else, and when I express my religious convictions I speak only for myself. Just as I have never tried to pressure my business associates to adapt their ideas to my way of thinking, I would never insist that another believer look at the Bible as I do. I respect people with convictions and wish that more people would develop them.

There are many different interpretations about the Kingdom age. I would hesitate to say that any one of them is right or wrong, because the Bible gives us only a sketchy outline of the life that lies in the future. The only interpretation I would reject is the one that is not based upon a belief that the Bible is the inspired Word of God and that therefore it is without error.

My approach to Bible study is not necessarily the right one for all believers, but I do think that each believer should have some approach. The future of eternity represents the ultimate purpose of God in dealing with the human race He created with Adam and the spiritual race He created with Jesus Christ, and in order to understand what goes on in the world today we need to understand that purpose. Before businessmen can analyze a problem, select personnel to do the job, and work out operating plans, they have to ask themselves what they want to accomplish, or as Peter Drucker puts it, "What kind of business are we in?" When they have that clearly in mind, the other things begin to fit into place. It is the same with us in solving the problems of life. As we grow and mature, deciding how to use our time, our abilities, and our opportunities, we should try to understand God's ultimate purpose for man and see where it applies to our lives. A study of the second coming of Christ is vital to each of us, and if we know what it means, we can be among those who wait and watch.

18

Living
on God's Terms

No one can possibly appreciate the benefits he can
receive from the Bible until he has begun to understand
its message. Then, it is not a matter of what a man does
with the truth but what the truth does with him. For
one thing, it changes his life. Although each believer
will change in a different way, according to his personal history and present situation, all will find that life
becomes a new experience.

A person in the grip of fears, whether physical or
psychological, can find help from the Bible. People fear
all kinds of things these days and some live in an hour-
by-hour state of dread. Some are afraid to go to work
because they think they might get fired; some are
afraid to try because they might fail; some are reluctant
to speak because they are afraid people will laugh at
them; and some live in the constant fear that they
might lose the love of someone dear to them. I knew a
person who was afraid of losing control of his emotions.
A lot of these fears are unwarranted, but that makes no
difference to the people who suffer under their torment.

A BUSINESSMAN LOOKS AT THE BIBLE

I have been watching an interesting development in a man I got to know through our business dealings. He is a capable man, but he has been torn apart by fears which are more evident to others than to him. He is afraid of being inadequate, of offending people, of not living up to all that is expected of him; while these fears are not justified, they are very real to him. What is even more distressing is that he is a strong Christian who believes in the Bible, which ought to make him less vulnerable to fear. Well, he believes in the Bible, but he doesn't completely accept its truth, and that makes the big difference. When a person accepts the Bible on God's terms, not his own, he begins to let it guide his life and he gains the strength to face life's dreaded things and exorcise its imaginary bugaboos. Somewhere inside him, my frightened business friend must realize that there is only one source of help for him, and as he matures I have noticed that he is turning again and again to the Bible, trying harder to accept it completely. One of these days he will get rid of his fears—and I have good reasons for my optimism.

Worry is something else that trips us up all the time. We worry about our families, our businesses, our position in society, and about every conceivable kind of misfortune that might happen to us. I don't say that a Bible reader will never worry about anything—because there is much in modern life to cause us healthy concern—but I do say that he will worry a lot less. As he grows in spiritual knowledge, he will gain the awareness that there is a supreme protective Power looking after him, and he will be able to accept life with serenity.

I speak from my own experience, because I know what it is to bend under the burden of worry. While I was still in my twenties, my father's health began to fail, and most of his business responsibilities fell upon me. Then, along came the deep business recession of the early thirties, the bank closings, and the tough problems of keeping a business going when no one wanted to buy our merchandise. I worried myself into a pretty sad state, upsetting not only myself but others around me, until I finally realized that I had to do something about it. I took a good long look at myself and at my difficulties, and I decided that worry wasn't going to help me solve them. Besides, I saw that some of the things that troubled me were beyond the realm of reality and wouldn't happen in a million years. As far as the real problems were concerned, I decided that I could do no more than my very best and I would simply have to take the consequences, good or bad. I made up my mind that I would never worry again, but I made the decision on the basis of my faith in God. I realized that if I really believed that God loved me, and that He was all-powerful, I was actually insulting God by allowing myself to get worked up into a state of anxiety.

I made that decision over thirty years ago, with God's help, and I can positively say that I have not worried since then. When I could approach my problems with confidence instead of desperation, I found many new ways to solve them, and I began to understand that man's anxiety over his human helplessness is the thing that most often defeats him—in business or in any other area of his life. When I say that I do not worry today, I do not mean that I am numb to life. I am concerned about many matters, I have put forth strenuous personal efforts in coping with many situations, and I have known disappointment. But I go to sleep quickly when I hit the bed at night, and I am physically relaxed during the day, because I am conscious of being under the watchcare of the Holy Spirit of God. I believe this awareness is available to everyone who accepts God's Word, and this is not my own idea—I learned it from the Bible.

The Bible is the best self-help Book in the world, and it can help you reduce your shortcomings. It can throw light on your weaknesses and faults and show you how to do something about them. Of course, if you begin to concentrate on your own faults, you won't have the time or the inclination to look for them in someone else, so that is an added benefit. To those who seem to enjoy criticizing others and complaining about the world—which is neither the route to popularity nor very healthy—I would also recommend the Bible, for it would give them a new outlook on life.

There are days in every life when things do not look bright, when it is easy to become discouraged, and when even our best efforts do not produce good results. These are the times to seek help from the Bible. If you read it regularly, it will give you a new outlook, an encouraging uplift, a boost for your morale, and you will know fewer periods of depression.

As long as we are in the flesh and in this dispensation, none of us is going to be absolutely sinless, but that doesn't mean that we should give way to vice. It is our job to fight against the weakness of the flesh, but we won't get very far on our own strength. It is amazing how many people are enslaved by sins, by habits of vice, which they want to overcome and yet cannot find the strength to do it. They are like an acquaintance of mine who had no place in his life for spiritual matters but all the time in the world for so-called pleasures. After a while, the pleasures began to eat away at his life, breaking up his family and dissipating his prosperity, until he realized that, like the prodigal son, he had to take stock of himself. For the first time he began to think about his relationship with God, and when he started to read the Bible he saw how futile his old life had been. As long as he ran on his own steam he went steadily and rapidly downhill. Call it coincidence, if you will, but when this man allowed the Bible to guide him to the strength of God, his life began to change. He began to repair its broken pieces and today he is a much richer man, not only in material things. His greatest prosperity is his new revelation of God's power in his life.

Great things are in store for the person who overcomes himself, and if this experience happens to only a few of us it is not God who sets the limitations, but our human nature. God is incredibly generous. To all His children He would give vast spiritual joys and riches, a deeper understanding of life, and resources to meet its problems—but there are few takers.

Some people may hold back from the Bible because they do not understand how such a complex Book can be of any practical help in their lives. They point to the everyday problems that all of us face—the job, the family, getting along with people—and they wonder where the Bible fits into that kind of picture. I think it fits in very well. Since all the areas of our lives are interrelated, trouble in one area is likely to upset the others. If our physical bodies are out of order, it affects our spirit, our mental outlook, our ability to cope with life, and the same chain reaction takes place when we neglect our spiritual health. We can achieve a sound spiritual well-being through taking daily nourishment from the Bible.

If a businessman is going to be effective, he must be realistic, practical, openminded, and a good judge of values. When he buys materials to be processed or merchandise to be resold, he must be able to prove to his own satisfaction that he can honestly recommend them to others. A man who owns a restaurant must be convinced that his food is so good that he eats it himself, and a clothing manufacturer must have enough faith in his products to wear them.

I apply these same principles to everything in life, and especially to the Bible. I have read it, studied it, believed it, and applied it in my own life, and I can recommend it to everyone because it is worth the price. I believe it deserves your most careful consideration.

If you have lived according to man's wisdom, you have a good idea of what it offers. Why not try living according to God by letting the Holy Spirit speak to you through His Book? You will find it offers far more benefits than those I have mentioned. Jesus said that He came that we might have life and have it more abundantly, and perhaps this is the best description of the new life that you will discover. The spiritual rebirth is so far beyond our human understanding that you will begin to know what it means only when you live it, when you feel the embryo within you beginning to grow. Then you will experience a new internal joy, a readiness to meet life's burdens, and a willingness to look toward the future with serenity and assurance.

Maxey Jarman